Y0-BOE-479

HUNTERS OF SOULS

Saint Dominic receives the rosary.

11188 SE 27th Ave.
BRINK'S
Milwaukie, OR 97222

HUNTERS OF SOULS

DOMINICAN SAINTS AND BLESSED

SISTER MARY JEAN DORCY, O.P.

THE NEUMANN PRESS

LONG PRAIRIE, MINNESOTA

Nihil obstat: GULIELMUS S. MORRIS, S.S., Censor Deputatus
Imprimatur: † GERALDUS SHAUGHNESSY, S.M., Episcopus Seattlensis
2 Julii, 1946

Hunters of Souls

The Neumann Press
©1999 Edition
Original edition 1946

ISBN   0-911-845-87-9

PRINTED AND PUBLISHED IN THE UNITED STATES OF AMERICA
THE NEUMANN PRESS, LONG PRAIRIE, MINNESOTA 56347

TO M. M. F.

UNDER THE PATRONAGE OF
THE "HUNTERS OF SOULS"

FRANCIS AND DOMINIC

Acknowledgments

To my Brothers and Sisters in Saint Dominic, whose inspiration and assistance have made this work possible, my most sincere thanks.

Contents

[7]

Preface to Boys and Girls

YOU do not remember a time when there were no airplanes, no trains, no radios, no automobiles, refrigerators, telephones, or motion picture shows. Even your mother and father are so used to all these things that it is hard for them to remember there ever was a time when things were different. But you know, if you think hard enough, that people did not always dress the same as they do now, or live in the same kind of houses, or travel in the same way, or play the same games. You have read stories about them and seen pictures of them, and perhaps these people of long ago seem very strange to you. Would you be surprised to find that boys and girls of seven hundred years ago were not so very different from boys and girls of today?

The boys and girls whose stories are told in this book grew up to be saints. That is what we all must grow up to be if we wish to go to heaven. It is not true that "all the saints lived and died a long time ago, and things were different then." Sanctity is always in style, and you and I must be saints too. It is to help boys and girls of today to get acquainted with these boys and girls of yesterday that this book is written. When you read it you will see that airplanes, trains, and radios do not make any real difference. Children like the same things today that children liked hundreds of years ago. And it is just as hard to be good as it ever was.

All the saints in this book lived long ago, before our United States was even dreamed of. Some of them lived before Columbus discovered America. Only three lived in the New World, because the New World at that time was still a wilderness, and the white man had not even begun to build our country. People did not know then many of the facts of science and geography and medicine that we know today. (We must not think they were stupid, however; for they knew many things that we have forgotten.) And the saints who lived in these long-ago days went to heaven by the same pathway we must use today — by obeying God's laws.

Sadly enough, we do not know all that we would like to know about those wonderful people, the saints. It is strange about grownups: they never seem to write down the important things — and there are many things about the childhood of the saints we should like very much to know, but do not. However, we do know one big thing about all these saints: They went to heaven because they loved God enough to keep His laws. When you learn how they did it, you will want to do the same; and may God bless you and give you the courage to do it.

From a Castle in Spain

THE boy with two greyhounds on his leash stopped just at the edge of the forest and pulled back steadily on the two straps. He had a strong wrist for a boy of seven, but he still had to brace himself against a tree root to stop the two dogs. "We mustn't go into the woods, Prince," he said. "Come back, Lady. Some other time. It's getting dark down here in the valley, and we have to go home. See," he said, as he heard the sound of a horn from the hill above them, "there's Mannes out looking for us already."

He took a small silver-mounted horn which hung at his side and blew an answering note. The echoes drifted back to him from the hill. There was an answering note from his brother's horn, and then a number of short blasts. "News! It's news from Father!" cried the boy. He stopped just long enough to answer with another blast from his own horn; then with the two dogs in the lead, he started scrambling up the path. He arrived at the gate of the castle quite breathless, to find Mannes as excited as he. "What news?" he cried. "Is Father home?"

"Not home, but coming home," said his brother. "*Where* have you been, Dominic?" He unleashed the two dogs, and they went scampering off while he sat down beside his little brother. "The messenger came just an hour ago. He said that Father will be here day after tomorrow. They have defeated the Moors in the place where they were fighting, and they hope there will be no more trouble for a while."

"My, but I hope Father can stay home this time," said Dominic. "You know, Mannes, I've only seen him twice. He is always away fighting the Moors."

"I hope he will stay, too," said Mannes, "but that is the work of Christian knights — to fight the Moors, and protect Spain and holy Church. Father is needed here at the garrison; but he is such a brave soldier that they need him more on the field, I guess."

"He can tell us all about the battles," said Dominic, his eyes shining with excitement. "Mother told me how Saint James rides out to battle on a white horse, with a banner in his left hand and a drawn sword in his right, when the Christian troops are losing. Then they all cry, 'Saint James and Spain to battle!' and he helps them win. But it will be

"We mustn't go into the woods, Prince," he said.

even better to hear Father tell it. Do you suppose he will have time?"

"I don't know, Dominic," said Mannes. "But maybe you will be going out to see the world yourself one of these days, and then you'll have stories of your own to tell."

Dominic looked at his brother. "You mean — I'm going away?" he asked.

"Every Spanish nobleman sends his son away for an education," said Mannes. "You know that. And now you are seven, and it is time for us to be thinking about your future."

Dominic looked up soberly at the castle keep, the square ugly tower of stone that was just in front of them. For just a moment there was a lump in his throat when he thought of leaving Calaroga, and he remembered what he would be leaving. There was his lovely, gracious mother, Lady Joanna; the tall soldier-father he saw so seldom; his brothers, Anthony and Mannes; the old parish church of San Sebastian; and the tiny chapel of Saint George on the rock above the castle; all his friends of the garrison, and the two greyhounds he had been so proud to train. "Do you know where I'm going?" he asked Mannes.

His brother was slow to answer. "Mother isn't sure," he said. "You know, she always thought that you would be a knight like Father, and live on here at the castle, since Anthony and I are both going to be priests. But now she thinks that you, too, should have a chance to study for the priesthood. You have done very well with your lessons and you like books. You know, we have an uncle who is a priest in the cathedral at Gumiel d'Izan. I think it quite likely that you will be sent there to study under his care."

"I'd like that," said Dominic, rising. "I think I'll go find Mother."

Lady Joanna de Guzman was busy in the pantry, checking the food on hand with some of the servants. "We will want the best of everything when Master Felix comes home," she was saying. "He is very tired from the long wars, and we must give him the best we have." She looked up to see Dominic standing in the doorway, the greyhounds on either side of him. For a minute she remembered a dream she had had, years ago, about Dominic. She had seemed to see him, running like a swift greyhound through the world, with a blazing torch in his mouth. Wherever the torch touched, fire flamed up. She did not know what the dream might mean, except that Dominic must be chosen by God to do something very special in the world. "Come in, my little hunter," she said with a smile. "We have just time for a little walk before sunset." She put a hand on his shoulder and they went out the door together. "What were you hunting?" she asked.

"Nothing very much, Mother. I think we were just racing, because it is so nice to be out in this spring weather," he said.

"Perhaps you are going to be a hunter of souls," she said. "Would you like that, Dominic?"

"Are there many souls to hunt for, Mother?" he asked. "Besides the Moors, I mean?"

"Let us walk up on the east battlements so we can see if a messenger comes," she said instead of answering. They climbed the steep path to the walk around the east tower of the castle, and stood there looking down into the valley of the river. That river, Dominic knew, was the boundary between the Moors and Christian Spain. Now it sparkled so peacefully in the fading sunlight that no one would ever dream it had often run red with blood. He looked south over the treeless land to where mountains gleamed pink in the setting sun. To the north were more mountains, but these were already shadowy.

Dominic looked at the mountains with a little frown on his face. "You know, Mother," he said, "when I was very little I used to think those mountains were at the edge of the world. Ever since you told me they weren't, and that there were people on the other side, I have wanted to go and see. And if they are people who have never heard of God, that is all the more reason why I should go to them. Was that what you meant when you said there were many souls to hunt?"

Lady Joanna was about to answer when she saw, far down the road that came from the east, a cloud of dust rising. "Do you suppose that could be Father already?" asked Dominic eagerly. She did not answer, but they watched the dust cloud as it rolled closer across the plain. Finally she shook her head. "They are pilgrims," she said, "on the way to the shrine of Saint James at Compostella."

"But that must mean that the roads are open and the Moors defeated," he said. "Oh, Father will be home soon! Won't that be wonderful?"

But Dominic was not to see his father so soon. At dawn a messenger arrived at the gates of Calaroga with his disappointing message. There was more trouble with the Moors — this time, to the south. Felix de Guzman would not be home for months, perhaps not for years. So it was Lady Joanna who took Dominic to Gumiel d'Izan to start his lessons under the care of his uncle.

Life at Gumiel d'Izan was very exciting for a boy who had lived all his seven years in a small castle far from the cities, with only the pilgrims passing to and from the shrine to keep him in touch with the outside world. Dominic was a good student; but studying Latin, learning to serve Mass, and memorizing the Psalms would not keep a bright boy busy all the time, and Dominic found a great deal to see and do. Many times visiting priests or bishops would stay at his uncle's house on the way to or from the shrine of Saint James. They came from all sorts of strange places, countries he had never dreamed of. Sitting quietly in the corner while they talked, Dominic heard their stories of faraway lands and strange peoples.

Some came from Italy and they talked of Rome. Some had been to Jerusalem and the shrines of the Holy Land. He saw jewels, spices, pieces of shining silk and gold-embroidered cloth that knights had brought back from the Crusades. Somewhere east of Jerusalem, they said, was the kingdom of spices and of great wealth. Traders came from there to the Holy Land, on camels like those the Three Kings had brought to Bethlehem, to sell their goods to the crusaders from the west.

Dominic listened wide-eyed while the priests from Hungary and Poland told of the cruel Tartars who rode down out of the north on their swift ponies, spreading death and terror wherever they went. "There," thought the little boy, "are people who really *need* to be told about God. When I grow up I am going to be a missionary, and I'll go to the Tartars to teach them about God and His laws."

Sometimes Dominic would be sent on an errand into the town. On market days, when the narrow streets were crowded with shouting people selling their wares, the small boy from Calaroga watched and listened with a sinking heart. Here were souls, thousands of them, he supposed; and how many of them acted as though they had ever heard of God? It had begun to look as though the whole world needed to be told about God and His Blessed Mother, about honesty and kindness and purity!

Dominic had quite firmly decided to be a priest by the time he was fourteen, so he was sent to the city of Palencia to go to higher school. Here he was hard at work on his books when one day sad news came. The Moors had made another attack, and had pushed into Spain almost as far as Palencia itself. Frightened and starving people poured into the town. Dominic, going from church to school, would meet them on the streets begging for something to eat. Since he had already given away everything he could spare, he had nothing left to give. But the cries of the suffering people rang in his heart so loudly, that one day he gathered up his precious books and sold them so he could give the money to the poor refugees to buy bread.

This was a big sacrifice for a boy who was going to school. Not only did each book cost so much he could not buy another, but also he would have to write new textbooks for himself if he wanted to keep up with his studies. "But," he said, "I can't study from dead skins when living people are crying for food."

Dominic studied quietly for ten years, and when he was twenty-five he was ordained a priest at the cathedral of Osma in Spain. He was very happy to be able to say Mass at last. People who watched the young priest at the altar remembered the story they had heard about a star appearing on Dominic's forehead when he was baptized. When he said Mass his face was so bright with happiness that it almost seemed as if the star were still shining.

Dominic had never forgotten his dream of going to preach to the Tartars. He was busy enough at the cathedral, chanting the Office and working among the people, that he need not look for anything else to do. But he could not forget those millions of pagan souls out there in the darkness on the other side of the mountains. Sometimes he thought of the poor refugees in Palencia crying for bread, and he thought that he heard the Tartar people crying for the bread of eternal life. He made up his mind that if ever he had the chance, he would leave Spain and go away to the north to look for souls among the Tartar tribes.

The chance came about in a strange way. His bishop, Diego, sent for him one day. "I must go to Denmark to arrange a royal marriage," he said. "I would like you to come with me."

Father Dominic was very glad to go. It was true, their

road did not lie through Hungary, but through France; still it was north. They started the long journey very happily. There were many things to see. On the road they met people from many different lands. Their languages were all different, but all spoke enough Latin to visit with each other when they met on the road.

France was very beautiful; but as they went along, they saw that something was wrong. Castles were ruined; the small homes of peasants, burned; fields, blackened and deserted. It could mean only one thing — war. "It is the heretics and the Catholics who are fighting," explained people they met on the road. "There are many heretics here. There is much suffering."

These heretics, Dominic knew, were people who had been Catholics, but, for some reason, had gone wrong in their beliefs. They believed not in one true God, but in two gods: one good and one evil. That made it easier to blame all their own sins on the evil god. They did not believe in many things Catholics must believe, and they did not love our Blessed Mother. He knew there had always been a few people who liked to believe foolish things, but he was surprised that people followed their teachings. It was a pity to see so many losing their souls. The heretics had caused just as much ruin in the souls of the people they had led astray as they had caused to the countryside in burning and killing. Dominic and Bishop Diego were very sad as they went along and saw the burned houses and the ruined fields.

One night they stayed at an inn where the innkeeper himself was a heretic. Dominic talked to him to find out what his beliefs were so he could correct them. They talked and talked — and after everyone else had gone to bed, they kept right on talking. In fact, they talked all night! But by morning the man had given up the foolish teaching of the heretics, and was once more a good Catholic.

Even after they had gone on to the north, Dominic could not forget the heretics. "They need someone to help them, too," he said. "They would not believe lies if someone were near to tell them the truth. That is what the whole world needs — the truth about God and His laws. The Tartars need it, and the Moors need it, and the heretics need it; even the ordinary people in the towns need it! How true are the words of our Lord, 'The harvest indeed is great, but the laborers are few'!"

The marriage was arranged, and they came back to Spain. Then for the second time, Bishop Diego and Dominic and the rest of the party started north, this time to bring the Danish princess home to Spain to her royal bridegroom. But when they reached her father's castle, sad news awaited them. The princess had just died. They started on the long road back to Spain.

On the way back to Spain, both Bishop Diego and Dominic wanted to stop for a while in France to work among the heretics. "If they only knew the truth, they would not believe lies!" said Dominic. So they and a few other priests began giving missions among the heretics. They went among them as poor people preaching the gospel of truth against the lies of the heretic leaders. They worked very hard, and had very little results. The heretic leaders were rich and powerful. When the time came that they had to go back to Spain, Dominic felt very sad at the thought that so many souls were still being lost in France.

After they returned to Spain, Bishop Diego and Dominic took the road to Rome. There they asked the pope to let them go, as they had so long desired, to the Tartars. The pope shook his head. "France needs you more right now," he said. "Go back to France and stamp out the teachings of the heretics by teaching them the truth."

So back to France they went. A number of other priests joined them, also several Catholic men who wanted to help.

Dominic even founded a society among the Christian knights called the "Militia of Jesus Christ" whose members were pledged to work wherever they were needed against the heretics. But even so, it was very slow and discouraging.

For the heretics had one very good fighter on their side, and that was the devil. He was pleased to see souls believing in lies, for he deals in lies himself. That is really his business — to see that souls do not see the truth. And for a time it looked as though he and his army would win out, at least with the heretics of France. That, of course, was before our Lady stepped into the battle.

There is a verse in the Scriptures which speaks of our Lady as:

> "Fair as the moon, bright as the sun,
> Terrible as an army in battle array. . . ."

To be sure, if the devil had remembered that she would be fighting against him, he might have turned tail and run before that. But it all happened so quietly, perhaps, that the devil, who isn't so smart after all, didn't notice. And before he knew it, he was beaten.

For it was only that Dominic was in church praying, which he often did. And he was praying so hard that his very heart was aching. "Those souls, Blessed Mother of God, those thousands of souls are being lost!" he pleaded. "Lost, and the Precious Blood of your Son was shed for them, too. Lost because they can't, or won't, see the truth. Queen of Heaven, you *must* help these people!"

And there before his very eyes, so the legend says, a bright, bright cloud was shining. In the cloud was a Lady so lovely that no one need ever ask who she was. Only the Queen of Heaven could look like that. Only her Blessed Son could be as lovely as the Babe she held in her arms.

Dominic's heart nearly stopped beating. "What will you have me do, Mother?" he asked.

"Teach them my rosary." She smiled, and he thought

all heaven was opened before him. Then the vision disappeared.

So he taught the rosary. There had been many ways used before this, of counting prayers with little pebbles or beads. But legend tells us that it was Dominic who first taught people to think about the fifteen mysteries, and so spread far and wide the love of our Lady and the rosary. Before that terrible "secret weapon" which held fifteen Our Fathers, one hundred and fifty Hail Marys, and the fifteen mysteries, the forces of heresy melted like snow. And the devil, who was always getting beaten by our Lady's interference, howled sadly to see thousands of souls turning from the heretics to listen to Dominic and his preachers.

The heretics liked to argue. They would challenge Dominic or some of his followers to come out on the public square and argue with one of their teachers. Everyone in town would come to listen. One day Dominic was arguing with a very stubborn heretic. "You are so sure that you are right, and I am so sure that I am right, I am afraid we will be days in reaching an agreement," he said. "Suppose you write what you believe on a piece of parchment, and I'll write what the Catholic Church teaches on another piece of parchment. Then we will put them in the fire, and perhaps God will show us which is the true belief."

They both did so, and a few days later a huge fire was built and the two parchments were thrown into it. That of the heretic blazed up and was aflame in an instant. Dominic's was thrown out of the fire, as though someone had tossed it out of the flames. They threw it in again, and again it was thrown out. Again and again they tried to burn it, but it would not even scorch. The heretic leaders were very angry, but many of the people were converted by the miracle.

One day when Dominic had just finished a sermon, a

Meeting of Saint Francis of Assisi and Saint Dominic.

group of nine young women came up and asked to see him. "We have been very wrong in our beliefs," they said. "And now we want to belong to the true faith. But if we become Catholics we do not dare go home because our parents are heretics. We want to spend our lives in prayer, and we certainly cannot do that at home."

"I must pray for help to know what to tell you," said Dominic. He did so, and several days later he called them to him. "I will make you into a community of sisters," he said. "You will be shut away from the world by what is called a 'cloister.' You will wear a certain type of dress which we call a 'habit.' You will pray, and teach, and spin wool, and weave cloth and embroider, and do other good things. Most of all, you will pray for me and for the other preachers who are trying so hard to teach people the truth."

Soon after this, Dominic went to Rome to see the pope. He explained to the pope about the priests who were working with him, and about the need for preachers to teach people the truth. "I would like your blessing on my new Order," he said. "We want your permission to preach to all the world. We believe that if people only knew the truth they would never believe lies. This Order I would like to start would be made up of preachers and teachers who would first study very hard to learn exactly what the Catholic Church believes, and then go out and teach it to all the people of the world. Our motto would be *Truth*."

While he was in Rome, so the old legends say, he met another man who was there for the same reason he was. His name was Francis, and he came from Assisi in Italy. He wore a brown habit with a white cord tied around the waist. "Money and the greed for money are to blame for many souls being lost," Francis said. "I and my followers will preach love of God and poverty." Whether they really met in Rome no one seems to know; but the two holy men were great friends.

When the pope had given his permission for the new Order of Preachers, Dominic went back to France and called all his followers together. There were sixteen: eight Frenchmen; seven Spaniards, among whom was his own brother Mannes; and one Englishman. In the cloister, where he had placed the nine young women, were now a group of sisters to pray for the success of their preaching. Because Dominic had worn white when he was at the cathedral of Osma, he still wore a white habit and a black cloak. The sisters had the same except that they wore veils, as all ladies of the time wore veils of some sort.

As Dominic stood before his little group on the day he had called them together, they all wondered what he was going to say to them. He said many things, probably something like this: "We are going to preach to the whole world, my sons. The world is in darkness and in need of truth. You are not monks to live in a convent away from the world; you are friars, and friar means 'brother.' You are brothers to all the world's peoples. Go, now, and search out souls for Christ." Then he told each where he was to work: some to Spain, some to Paris — two and two, he sent them out like the Apostles of long ago. "The seed must be scattered if it is to grow," he said. "It will mold if we leave it heaped up in the bin."

A short time proved that Dominic was right in scattering his preachers; for in two years there was not one convent only, but sixty. In these, thousands of young men were eagerly studying to be like their model, Dominic — a teacher, a missionary, and a saint. Young men left home, wealth, and pleasure to throw themselves at the feet of Dominic and beg to be admitted to his Order. Once trained in the rule of the Order, they went out to preach — north, south, east, west. Some went to the Moors, and shed their blood to bring them the truth. Some worked among the heretics in Christian Europe. Some went to Hungary, where Dominic himself had always wanted to go, to the Tartars, and died there as the first martyrs of the north. Some followed the trade routes to the east; and in a short time after Dominic's death, they were to reach around the known world.

In the little time left of Dominic's life on earth, much was to happen. One thing was the coming into the Order of two very great men who later were to be beatified by the Church: Jordan of Saxony and Reginald of Orleans. Because Reginald's story is a story of our Lady's love for the Order, it must be told.

Reginald was a young priest when he met Dominic and begged to join the Order. Dominic had barely said yes, and Reginald was not yet even wearing the white habit of the Order when he became very sick; and everyone thought he was going to die. Dominic loved him very much, and he was sad to think that Reginald was going to die; so he prayed for his recovery if it should be God's will. And God sent His own Mother, so the legend says, to make Reginald well. She not only cured the sick priest, but she also showed him a garment made of white wool. "See, this is the habit of your Order," she said. "This scapular you should always wear." So it was that the scapular, as well as the rosary, are parts of the Dominican habit that remind us of our Lady's love.

Reginald and Jordan were very dear friends of Dominic. There were many others among his early followers who were later called saints or blesseds by the Church. Dominic himself worked so many miracles that it would take a very big book to tell them all.

In spite of all the hard work he did, Dominic was never easy with himself. His penances were very great; he fasted much and prayed sometimes all night, sleeping only for a few minutes with his head on the altar steps. He kept nothing for himself, and his habit was old and mended. He would not even allow himself to ride on any of his long journeys across Europe. He walked along from city to city singing or chanting the Psalms. In spite of all that might have made him sad, he was very happy. He took nothing with him but a staff, his prayer book, and a copy of the Bible.

When his time came to leave this earth and go to heaven, Dominic's followers gathered sadly around him. They were all crying, or at least complaining that he was leaving them. Dominic did not like this at all, for he was above all a cheerful man and he did not like long faces. "Don't feel so sad," he said. "I am leaving you just for a little while. You will soon join me, for life is short. And I will be of more use to you in heaven than I ever was on earth. Behold, my children," he went on, "the heritage I leave you: guard humility, have charity for one another, make your treasure out of voluntary poverty."

More than anything else in the life of Saint Dominic, we remember his preaching of the truth and his love for our Lady Queen of Heaven. This love he has passed on to all his Dominican children in their love for the rosary. Today every Catholic says the rosary, and few remember who it was that first spread in the world this great devotion. At Lourdes, six hundred years after Saint Dominic's time, our Lady appeared again to remind people to say this, her favorite prayer.

For many years the followers of Dominic were called "Friars of Mary" because of their love for the rosary; or "Preaching Friars" because of their work; or, finally, "Dominicans" after the name of their founder. Today they are all around the world preaching in every mission field, in lands not discovered or even dreamed of in Saint Dominic's day.

How happy Dominic must be up in heaven to see that his dreams are coming true, of truth being brought to all the peoples of the earth. One man could never hope to go to everyone — Moors, Tartars, heretics, pagans — that his heart had ached to save. But his Order has carried to the far parts of the earth the sparks from that flaming torch of truth, which once he carried blazing through the world.

The Creed of a Boy Named Peter

PETER shifted his copybook to the other arm and made a deep bow. "Good afternoon, Uncle," he said. "Were you on your way to our house to visit?"

The tall man in the red cloak turned and looked down at his little nephew. "Well, well," he said cheerfully, "if it isn't Peter. Coming home from school?"

"Yes, Sir," Peter answered.

"And how are you getting along in school, my boy?" asked his uncle, turning to walk down the street with him. "You're the wisest boy in Verona, I suppose?"

"Oh, no, Sir," said Peter. "I'm getting along all right, I think. But it takes time."

"That's right," the man said with a broad smile. "It takes time. Well, Peter, exactly what *have* you learned? Can't you recite something for me, so I'll know you aren't just wasting your time at that school?"

"Oh, it's not a waste of time, Uncle, truly it isn't," said Peter. "I can say the 'Credo' for you if you like."

"Very well," said his uncle.

"I believe in God, the Father Almighty," Peter began, "Creator of heaven and earth, and . . ."

"No, no — wait a minute!" cried his uncle. "That isn't right, Peter. God didn't make this world."

"Oh, yes He did, Sir," said Peter, "and He made everything in it."

"Is that what they teach you over at that school?" asked his uncle, frowning. "Why, that's nonsense. I'll soon teach you better. Now you listen to me. . . ."

Peter listened while his uncle talked on and on. He was too polite to interrupt an older person talking; but he was too smart to believe what he knew was not true, no matter how good it sounded when his uncle said it. For Peter knew that his uncle, like many people of that time, was a heretic; that is, he did not believe in the true teachings of the Catholic Church. Peter's own father and mother were heretics, and believed all the wicked or silly things that his uncle would tell them. He had heard it all before. But, perhaps because God very early gave him the grace to believe only the truth, it made no impression on him at all. So he listened politely to his uncle until he was ready to stop.

"There, now," said his uncle. "That's the real truth. Now what do you believe?"

Peter stood up very straight and looked into his uncle's face. "I believe in God, the Father Almighty, Creator of heaven and earth," he said again; and before his uncle could stop him, he had said all the rest of the prayer.

"You're hopeless," cried his uncle. "I'll have to talk to your father about you!" So he strode off to find Peter's father, leaving the boy in the street.

"I do believe in God," Peter said to himself. "I do believe He created heaven and earth. I do believe that He loves me. If Father beats me for believing that, I will just have to take a beating, because I believe it with all my heart, and nothing can make me change if God helps me."

He went into the house just in time to hear his uncle saying to his father, "I tell you, if you don't take that boy out of the Catholic school, you never *will* be able to teach him our ideas."

"Who, Peter?" asked his father, laughing "Oh, no. That

boy is too young to know what it's all about. I wouldn't worry about him. He'll soon forget it all."

Peter went slowly up the stairs, thinking hard. "Even if I am little," he said to himself, "I'm big enough to know that God made me — to know Him, to love Him, and to serve Him in this life so that I can be happy with Him forever in the next. And I have to stand up for that belief, even when it hurts. God is my Father, and He knows I am little. He will help me to be brave. He gave me a guardian angel, and a Blessed Mother, and a brave patron saint to help me. Nobody is strong enough to fight against *them!*

In the years when he was in school, Peter had need of all the help he could get from his heavenly friends. Because there were so many temptations around him, he learned to pray a great deal for help, asking God and our Blessed Lady to keep his heart pure. His own family teased him, laughed at him, punished him, argued with him; but nothing could make him change his belief in the one true God. And while he prayed so hard for God's help, no one could talk him into sin.

He must have thought very often of the great Saint Peter for whom he was named. He knew that Peter had denied our Lord, but afterward had been sorry and spent his whole life in working for Jesus. In the end, he had given up his life for the Master he loved. So Peter, the "Rock" on which the Church was built, was a good patron for a boy who needed to be brave. Little Peter must often have prayed, "Help me to be strong and brave like you, Saint Peter, so that I won't be afraid to die for Jesus if I am asked to."

When Peter was fifteen, he was sent away to the University of Bologna to study. Here he met hundreds of other boys of his own age and older, who were studying (or should have been studying) like himself. But — perhaps it was because boys then were not so very different from boys nowadays — some of them didn't study at all.

They played truant from classes, and gambled and fought and got themselves into all sorts of trouble.

It isn't easy to be good when most of the people around you are bad, and Peter found that out very quickly. But instead of feeling sorry for himself and saying, "Oh, what's the use! Why should I behave myself when nobody else does?" he did what he had learned to do when he was only a little boy — he went to our Lady and *prayed* for help. And our Lady, who loves to help people be good, kept his heart pure in spite of the influence of others around him.

One day there was great news in the town. The boys whispered about it in class, and talked about it at lunch, and argued over it after school. A great preacher, whose name was Dominic, had come to town; and everyone in Bologna, it seemed, wanted to hear him. Peter along with many other boys, went to hear the saint preach.

After the sermon, as Dominic was making his way through the crowd in the street, he had to stop because there was someone kneeling right in front of him. It was a handsome young boy, and he was asking to be a friar like Dominic. "What is your name, my son?" asked Dominic.

"Peter, Master, and please let me come with you!" he answered. Dominic smiled and took his hand. "Come with me," he said. And Peter, so happy he could hardly talk, went with the holy preacher to receive the black and white habit.

Brother Peter — for that is what he would be called in the Order — was a very obedient novice and a very happy one. He was with the few who knelt around the holy Father Dominic as he was dying, and heard him say to his weeping brothers:

"Behold, my children, the heritage I leave you:
Guard humility,

Have charity one for another,
Make your treasure out of voluntary poverty."

Our Lord gave the young novice this grace, and many others, to prepare him for the trials that were coming to him.

But God had great work for Peter to do. Before he could go to heaven himself, he must help others to get there. His way of doing this was to preach; and preach he did, up and down the length of Italy. Crowds came to hear him, and went away resolved to be good. Many heretics were brought back to the true faith by his preaching.

Sometimes Peter would debate with the heretics in the public square, just as Saint Dominic had done. One time when he was doing this, the sun was terribly hot. Someone cried out, "If your God is the one true God, at your prayer He will send us a cloud to take away this terrible heat." In order to glorify God, Peter prayed for a miracle. It took place then and there. A cloud formed over the heads of the crowd and kept them cool and comfortable for the rest of the meeting.

Many miracles were performed by Father Peter as he went preaching from town to town. So many people were cured of terrible sickness, or healed from their wounds, that the heretics wanted to put a stop to the miracles. They thought they could do this by playing a trick on Father Peter. One of their number came limping into the square where Father Peter was preaching, and begged for cure of a sickness which he only pretended. The priest saw that he was lying, so he said to him, "If you are really sick, I pray God to cure you; but if you are not, I pray that He will *make* you sick in order to heal your soul." The man fell to the ground in great pain; and seeing how wicked he had been, began begging for pardon. Father Peter laid his hands on the man's head and healed him. More people than ever were converted by this miracle. The heretics were very angry.

One winter evening, Father Peter came into the town of Ravenna to preach. All the houses were covered with snow, and the drifts were deep in the streets as he walked along looking for the church. Finally he found it, and called for the sacristan. After he had told the man who he was, he said, "I'd like you to ring the preaching-bell so all the people will know there is going to be a sermon tomorrow and will be ready to come."

"It's no use, Father," said the sacristan. "This is the coldest winter we have had in years. Nobody will come when the snow is so deep."

"You'd better ring it anyway," said Father Peter.

But the sacristan didn't. He was so sure that no one would want to sit in a cold church and listen to a stranger preach, that he didn't bother his head about it. In fact he had forgotten all about the visitor and had been in bed and asleep for several hours when there was a terrible pounding at the door. He hurried down to see what was the matter. There in the snowy street was a crowd of people who insisted on knowing why there was a light in the bell tower at this hour of night! Was the church on fire?

The sacristan ran out into the street to look. There, surely enough, was a bright torch burning in the bell tower, shining out like a lighthouse beacon in the dark. It kept burning in spite of all the snow that was blowing thick around it. Suddenly, he remembered something. "It's a sign to all of us," he said. "There is a great preacher among us, Father Peter by name, who is going to preach tomorrow. I didn't ring the preaching-bell because I thought it was too cold for anyone to come. But God must want us to know that Father Peter is very holy." And great crowds pushed through the snowdrifts the next day to hear Father Peter preach.

[33]

At another time, Father Peter went to visit a knight who lived in a great castle. He had been a good friend to the priest, but now treated him very coldly. Father Peter soon saw the reason. The poor man had been tricked by the heretics and had fallen away from Catholic teaching. "What made you change your mind?" asked Father Peter. "You used to be a good Catholic."

"Yes, I used to be," said the man, "and I thought then that I was right. But one day I went to a meeting with these friends of mine (heretics) and our Lady appeared to me and scolded me for not believing as they do. She said she would forgive me if I would join their church and help them, so I did. It seems to me that if our Lady says they are right, they must be."

"That does seem reasonable," said Father Peter. "In fact, I'd like to see it myself. Could I go with you to one of your meetings?"

The knight was very happy to have Father Peter go with him for, he thought, "Now he will believe as we do, and stop bothering us with his preaching." So he told the priest yes; he could come with him the next morning.

But Father Peter wasn't fooled at all. He knew that our Lady had not really appeared to his friend; but that the devil, in order to steal his soul, had made himself look like our Lady and had lied to the people. So all night the good priest prayed very hard; and early in the morning before anyone else was up, he slipped away to a near-by church and said his Mass. There he consecrated two hosts (as the priest does on Holy Thursday); and, putting one into a little golden pyx, he hid it carefully under his clothes. Then he went back to the knight's home and the two of them set out for the heretics' meeting.

The heretics were all there; very pleased because Father Peter had come. They hoped to trick him into giving up his Catholic faith and joining them.

[34]

Once again, as they all watched, the devil took the form of our Lady before them; and everyone knelt down and cried out to her. That is, everyone but Father Peter. Instead of kneeling down, he was standing; and while they watched, something shining and gold glittered in his hand. Father Peter was holding up the pyx in which he had placed the Host, and his voice was like thunder as he cried out, "If you *are* the Mother of God, *adore your Son!*"

There was a terrible scream as the devil turned and ran, and the very wall of the church split open as he burst out. People screamed and fainted, and furniture crashed to the floor. For the devil could not stand to stay in the presence of the Blessed Sacrament; and there was nothing for him to do but run off pell-mell, howling in terror. And when things had quieted down, Father Peter preached to the people, bringing many of them back into the Catholic faith where they belonged.

After this, the heretics planned to kill Father Peter since they couldn't change his mind. They put their heads together and hired men to do the dreadful deed. Two men agreed to kill him for thirty pieces of silver. (Long, long before, an apostle sold his Master for the same amount.) so for weeks they shadowed Father Peter, watching everywhere he went and the times he went so they could get him alone and kill him.

Father Peter knew that his life was in danger. You might think it would frighten him, but it didn't. On the very day he was killed, as he and his companions were walking along the road to Milan, he began singing. It was Easter week and as they walked along singing Easter music, they thought of our dear Lord put to death on the cross for sinners. The two men who were planning to kill them lay in wait in the woods. As the priests came nearer, they could be heard singing. Little prickles of conscience began bothering one of the men, and suddenly he threw down his

*In his dying moment Father Peter wrote
his belief in God.*

knife. "I can't do it!" he said, and he turned and ran. But the other man's conscience did not bother him at all; he jumped out upon the two Dominicans and wounded them until he knew they would die.

A peasant plowing in a field near by heard the noise, and ran to see what had happened. He stopped in fright at what he saw — two men dying on the road, with blood staining their white habits and falling down into the sand. And what was it that one priest was doing? With his finger dipped in his own blood, he was writing on the sandy road. As he bent to help the priest, the peasant looked to see what he was writing. There were just four words: "I believe in God . . ." and then a broken line where Father Peter had grown too weak to write any more.

Today we call Father Peter "Saint Peter of Verona" or "Saint Peter Martyr." Since he is a saint in heaven, he can help boys and girls of our day to be faithful to their religious duties and strong in their faith. He will help those who pray to him to remain pure in body and mind; and to stay firm in the faith that is one, holy, catholic, and apostolic. His prayers will help us not only to die well, but also to live well. We may never be called upon to die for our faith as he was, though boys and girls in other lands than our own have had to do so; but we should pray to him to make our faith strong in these days of unbelief. He will help us to write in our own hearts, as he once did in the sands of a road nearly seven hundred years ago, "I believe in God"; so that our lives, like his, will lead others to heaven.

The Saint With the Seven-League Boots

"MOTHER, tell me some more about our Lady, Queen of Heaven," said Hyacinth, pulling his bench up closer to the huge fire. His brother Ceslaus, stretched out on the warm hearth, looked up and echoed, "Yes, mother, please do!"

"What shall I tell you this time?" asked their mother, turning her embroidery to fasten a thread. "I've told you all the stories I know about our Lady."

"But you could tell them all over again, and we wouldn't mind at all," said Hyacinth. "We like to hear about her, even if we've heard it before."

"I wonder if every child in the world has a mother to tell him stories about our Lady?" remarked Ceslaus, rolling over on his back and smiling up at his mother.

"No, I am afraid not, son," she answered him sadly. "One does not have to go far from our own land of Poland to find thousands who have never heard of our Lady or of her blessed Son."

Hyacinth sat up, his dark eyes wide and surprised. "Why doesn't somebody *tell* them, then?" he wanted to know.

Ceslaus laughed. "When he gets as old as I am, mother, he'll know it's not as easy as that," he said. "Why, Hyacinth, they don't *want* to hear about God. They'd rather fight. And they kill anyone who comes to them to teach them about God. Don't they, mother?"

"I'm afraid so," his mother agreed.

[38]

"When I grow up I'm going to go out hunting people who have never heard of God; and tell them all about Him, and about His Blessed Mother," said Hyacinth.

"That's a big job, Hyacinth," said his mother. "There are so *many* people who do not know God. One would hardly know where to begin. There are the Tartars and the Greeks and the Russians, and far away to the east, the Turks and the tribes of the Great Khan. They speak so many different languages, and they wander so far."

"Don't you suppose that our Lady would help you if you were teaching people about Jesus and about her?" asked Hyacinth.

"I'm sure she would," answered his mother with a smile. "She will never refuse to help you if you are faithful to her."

Small Hyacinth and his older brother were busy, as boys are apt to be. It might seem to us that there was very little for a boy to do in a big dark castle like that of their father, the Count of Odrowatz. There was, on the contrary, a great deal for two lively boys to do. There were fine horses to ride from their father's stables, also hawks and hounds for hunting. Every boy of that time must learn to shoot a crossbow, to use a sword, and to ride in armor; so these they must also do. They swam and wrestled and took part in races and contests, so that they grew strong and quick.

Athletics were not the only things they learned, for the count and countess wanted their children to be good Christians as well as strong men. The children often went with their parents to take food to the poor who came to the palace gates, or to visit them in their tiny homes. Hyacinth came to be a special favorite, for no one could help liking the sturdy little boy with the sweet smile, who seemed always to come visiting when people most needed to be cheered up.

Into the joy of their busy and noisy days came something — or rather, someone — who made a great deal of difference to Hyacinth and Ceslaus. That someone was their Uncle Yves, who was a priest in Cracow. He came for a visit to their father's castle; and when he went back to Cracow, he took his two nephews with him. They were smart boys, he said, and should have a chance to go to school. Far from the hunting and the carefree life at their father's castle, the two boys settled down to learn Latin.

Father Yves was so pleased with his two nephews that, after they had finished at Cracow, he sent them on to Prague and then to Bologna to study for the priesthood. There they were hard at work among their books for several years — hard at work, but not too hard to notice that the wild Tartars from the north were once more attacking Poland. They were both anxious to finish their studies so that they could go among these pagan tribes to preach the Gospel. They did not know that the chance to begin their work would come very soon.

Their uncle had been appointed a bishop, and must go to Rome to be consecrated. He sent for his two young nephews to go with him. They were very happy to have the chance to make such a trip. Travel at that time was not very pleasant (indeed, they had to walk all the way to Rome, and were at the mercy of wild beasts and bandits all the way), but it was still a great adventure for two young men who had never been to Rome.

As they went farther south on their journey, they were charmed by the birds and flowers, so much more plentiful there than in the cold north. The sight of the Alps filled them with great joy and awe at the majesty of God. And finally, on reaching Rome their hearts beat very fast with excitement.

Rome at that time was not exactly as it is today, for the dome of St. Peter's which we see in pictures was not built until some time later. Still, Rome was the heart of the

Christian world then as it is now; and, to the travelers from the north, everything was new and strange. Hyacinth and Ceslaus walked happily up and down the streets, visiting the churches and the tombs of the martyrs. It was while they were in Rome that they heard of Saint Dominic, the holy Spaniard whose preaching was leading so many into the service of God. They decided to go one day to hear him preach.

While they were on the way to the church to hear the great preacher a noise arose in the streets. People were shouting and running, and crying out in many languages. At first they could not tell what had happened, but as the crowd came nearer, they could see for themselves. A young man had fallen from his horse and was killed. His friends were weeping and shouting — afraid to take the news of his death to his family. Hyacinth and Ceslaus stood with their uncle in a doorway and watched the crowd coming down the street.

Suddenly the crowd parted, and a tall man in a white habit stepped into the circle around the dead boy. Those who were around him stepped back and looked at the stranger in surprise. "It's Dominic, the Spaniard," one person whispered to another. "The great preacher and miracle worker." The message passed from one person to another until it reached the three in the doorway. "There is Dominic, the preacher, now," said Father Yves. "The tall man in white. He looks like a saint."

"It would take a saint to do what he is doing," said Hyacinth. "With only a few companions, trying to preach to the whole world!"

"How I wish he and his preachers could come to Poland," said his uncle with a sigh. "Poor Poland — how the north needs missionaries!"

"Look," said Ceslaus, "he's having the dead boy brought into the church!"

They followed the crowd into the big church, and watched while the boy was laid before the altar; and Dominic went to vest for Mass. They prayed devoutly through the Mass, never taking their eyes from the saintly preacher at the altar. At the end of Mass, Dominic came down from the altar and spoke to the dead boy. "Arise, in the name of our Lord Jesus Christ!" And as they watched, the boy rose up — alive!

The people in the streets were so happy and so noisy, so busy cheering over the miracle, that the travelers from Poland could hardly push through to where the saint was standing. Once they reached him, they fell on their knees at his feet. "Your blessing, Father," they begged.

"We are travelers from the north," Father Yves explained, "and we came to you to beg you to send some of your preachers to our country of Poland."

Dominic's kind eyes looked very sad. "How my heart breaks to have to refuse you," he said. "But I have no one to go, no one at all. The Polish language is hard to learn, and not one of my few missionaries can speak it. But there must be *something* we can do. . . ." He looked down at Hyacinth and Ceslaus, and he knew their hearts were good. "Why do we worry? Here you have two fine young missionaries, right in your own family! Let them stay with me long enough to learn what the Preachers' life is, and then I will send them back to the north, wearing the white and black habit of our little mission band! Here, Father Yves, are your apostles of the north!" he said happily.

The two young men looked up at the saint, their eyes shining with happiness. "Do you really mean that you will let us join you?" they asked. "Why, the Preachers are saints — everyone says so!"

Dominic smiled and blessed them. "As soon as I can find habits for you, you may be my sons. Come!"

Hyacinth and Ceslaus were in Rome only long enough

to learn the Rule of the Friars Preachers, and to find out from the holy Dominic himself what their lives as Dominicans must be — poor, charitable, and pure. Then once again they took the road to Poland and the north. They walked along in happy silence, or singing hymns to our Lady, begging her to help them as they began their mission work. Somewhere in what is now Czechoslovakia, they came to a place where the road divided. They said good-by and went on — Brother Ceslaus and a companion going to Prague, Father Hyacinth and his companion going to Cracow.

Perhaps they never met again — no one thought to write it down whether they did or not. For two brothers who loved each other, it would be hard to say good-by for a lifetime; but that is part of a missionary's sacrifice. Then, too, they had now not just one brother apiece, but many brothers — for all over Europe more and more young men were joining the Friar Preachers, all religious brothers. And all over the frozen north, Hyacinth and Ceslaus worked to build more and more convents, where their brothers in Christ could live and praise God.

Hyacinth went first through his own country building new convents, receiving many young men into the Order. As soon as a convent was well started, he would go on to some distant city where he would preach and begin another convent. Soon there were many convents in Poland, and many Preaching Friars who went about teaching the people. Then, when his own country did not need him so much, he really began his travels.

We cannot imagine how anyone could travel as Hyacinth did, unless he really had the use of the famous seven-league boots! For with no other means of travel than by foot, he went through Pomerania, Prussia, Sweden, Norway, Denmark, Livonia, Moldavia, Lithuania, Russia, Indus, Thibet, Chinese Turkestan, and even faraway Tartary and China!

He sighted the great wall of China twenty years before Marco Polo saw it. If you will look at a map of Europe, even though many names have changed since his time, you will see what a lot of land he covered.

Remember, too, that hundreds of different languages were spoken in these countries. Also, almost all of them were pagan countries where no one had ever heard of kindness, or love, or purity, or peace as Christ taught it. There were wild forests to be crossed, and swollen rivers to be forded. Ice and snow and sleet must be suffered as well as the hate and greed of the pagans. Wild animals and bandits were the foes of every traveler. The hundreds of lonely miles between cities, Hyacinth walked alone. He made friends with the animals, watched the wild geese flying overhead, and thought of God who cares for all wild creatures.

We know that no man could travel as he did without help from heaven, and that Hyacinth had. As a little boy he had hoped to make our Lady known in the northland, and said that he would ask her help. She never failed him. Once at the very beginning of his missionary work, our Lady appeared to him at prayer and said to him, "You ask my help, my son. Be glad, for your prayer is answered. Everything you ask of God you will receive through me." Then, while Hyacinth watched, the heavens opened and she disappeared from his sight. But she kept her word; never did she refuse his prayers. Nor did Hyacinth ever forget to teach the people to love their Mother in heaven. He taught them to say the rosary; and wherever he went, he could be traced by the love for our Lady which he left with everyone who had heard him preach.

Once when he was preaching at Kiev in Russia, a great shout arose outside the church. "The Tartars are coming! They will burn the church!"

Hyacinth knew that was probably true, for the Tartars

*Saint Hyacinth saves the Blessed Sacrament and the
statue of our Lady.*

had burned every church they found. So he sent the people to safety, and went into the church to save the Blessed Sacrament. He was going out with the Blessed Sacrament safe under his cloak when he heard a voice calling, "Hyacinth, my son, Hyacinth, where are you going?"

He looked around hastily. Yes, the voice was really coming from the big statue of our Lady on the side altar. "I am saving the Blessed Sacrament from the Tartars," he answered.

"Hyacinth," said the voice sadly, "are you leaving my statue to be destroyed?"

"But it's so heavy, Blessed Mother!" said Hyacinth. "I couldn't carry it with two hands, let alone one."

"Try it and see," said the voice.

He did — and, wonder of wonders, the statue was as light as paper! "Take me with you always," said the voice. "My Son will lighten the load." Carrying his precious burden, Hyacinth passed safely out through the burning convent, and walked on top of the water across the river to safety.

At one time when Hyacinth was preaching in the north of Europe, he wished to build a convent on a rocky island at the mouth of the Vistula. Everyone objected. "It is too far from any city," said one. "It will be hard to get back and forth by boat all the time."

"You could not do any good there," said another. "Who would be near enough to hear the preachers?"

"It is still a good place for a convent," said Hyacinth. So finally they gave in and he built the convent on the rocky island. Some years later, the sea drew back, leaving the island connected with the mainland. A city grew up around the convent, and today that city — Danzig — is a very important city indeed.

Wherever Hyacinth went there were many miracles performed. In one place he gave sight to two boys born blind.

At another time he healed a woman whose tongue was paralyzed. Another time he raised to life a young man who had been drowned in crossing the river the day before. These and many more miracles made the people feel that he was near to God.

The devil, of course, did not like to be losing souls to this preacher. Once when Hyacinth was crossing a river, he saw an idol standing on an island. He stepped out of the boat, walked across the water, and broke the idol to bits. The devil appeared and called out to him, "Go away and let me alone! I was ruling here in peace until you came." Hyacinth took up a stick and chased the demon, then walked back across the water to the boat.

In all his travels, although Hyacinth took no one else with him, he was never alone. Not only his guardian angel, but our Lady herself was with him almost all the time. Some claimed that she was always beside him when he said his Mass; others said that when he was tired or discouraged, she comforted him. Once, at least, she appeared to dry his tears when he wept for the sins of men.

Hyacinth lived to be a very old man; and even when he was past seventy, he was still traveling, still preaching love of God and of our Lady. In his long life he had walked nearly twenty thousand miles through the wildest part of northern Europe, preaching the Gospel far and wide. At last he knew his time had come to die, and he went back to Cracow to die among his brothers there.

On the Feast of Saint Dominic in 1257, Hyacinth was just going up the altar steps to say his Mass when he saw a beautiful sight. All around the altar where he was to say Mass were shining angels; our Lady was there, and many saints, some of whom wore, like himself, the white habit of Saint Dominic. While he said Mass, the angels and saints looked on. When the Mass was finished, our Lady spoke to him, telling him to look up. There was such a light shining that he could hardly see, but there in the midst of the light was a crown made of stars and flowers. "Look," said our Lady, "this crown is for you!"

A few days later, on the Feast of the Assumption, Hyacinth died, and went off to heaven on our Lady's great feast to receive the crown of his works. Today, seven hundred years after his death, Saint Hyacinth is still remembered as the Apostle of the North, the missionary whose travels sound like a fairy tale. Remembering him, we should remember to pray for missionaries who in far lands are teaching today, and meeting hardships of all sorts that the world may be won for Christ. We should remember, too, that our work will be blessed as his was, if we do it always as he did, in the light of our Lady's smile.

Mother of the Poor

ZEDISLAVA (Zay-DEE-Sla-vah) is a hard name to say —
almost as hard, in fact, as "Rumpelstilzkin" and some of
those other fairy-tale names. But the lady whose name was
Zedislava was not a fairy-tale princess, even if she did live
in a castle long ago. Nor was it nearly as much fun living in
a castle as we might think it should be.

Zedislava's father was the commander of a fortified castle
on the frontier of Bohemia between the cities of Prague and
Vienna. It was the time when the Tartars were invading
Europe. Under his command were many soldiers, for they
had to defend an important road. At any hour of the day
or night an alarm might sound — "The Tartars are coming!
The Tartars are coming!" — and frightened people would
hurry to the shelter of the castle walls.

This meant that the castle had to be ready at all times
for battle. It meant, too, that there was little play for the
children of the commander. They learned very early that
when an alarm came even the smallest child had work to
do. It might be only to carry water or bandages, or to mind
the animals that the peasants had driven for safety into
the courtyard. Only the older boys, like Zedislava's two
brothers, could help to pass the ammunition to the men
who were fighting.

Zedislava and her sister Elizabeth might have envied
their brothers — if they had time to envy anybody — for

Blessed Zedislava learned early to be kind.

woman's work was hard and never seemed to end. Their mother, Lady Sybil, was careful to train her two little girls in all that they should know. It was woman's place to see that the castle storerooms were always full, and that the harvest was brought in at the right time and stored so that it would not spoil. She had to see that meats were smoked and spiced, wines made, and huge loaves of hard bread made and put away. Sheep must be sheared, wool spun, and cloth woven. Leather must be tanned for shoes, and furs trapped for winter clothing. While the lady of the castle did not do all these things herself, she had to see that they were done. For if war came when they were not ready, there would be much suffering.

In time of war one could not take time to worry about cooking food. All the women in the castle would be busy caring for the wounded, mixing medicines, bandaging, and seeing that food was sent to the fighting men. Even in peacetime there was much to do. Poor people came each day to the castle gate and the two little girls went with their mother to bring them food and clothing. "No one who is truly noble will ever refuse help to the poor," she told them over and over.

"But, mother," said Elizabeth one day as they walked down to the gate carrying big baskets of bread and fruit. "Everybody is not so kind to the poor as you are."

"We should not measure our kindness by other people's unkindness," said her mother. "Our dear Lord died for all of us, and He loves us all. If we are not kind to the poor, we are hurting Him."

"But there are so *many!*" said Elizabeth.

"That gives us just so many more chances to be kind," said Zedislava.

"Yes," said her mother, "and we should be very happy for having so many chances to earn heaven."

Little Zedislava was a favorite of the poor who came to

beg at her father's gate. Every day they watched for her to come out of the heavy gates with her arms full of good things for them, and a smile on her face. When she had time to stay, they gathered around her; and she taught them their catechism, or told them stories about the saints. If any were sad, it was she who cheered them or brought them some little gift. No matter how greedy or unpleasant a person might be, he could be sure of someone who would speak a kind word to him — and that someone was the smiling little daughter of Lady Sybil.

Zedislava tried to learn all she could that would make her useful to others. She learned what plants could be used for medicines and just how to mix them. She learned how to cook foods that sick people would like, and how to bandage and care for the wounded. When Lady Sybil called in the children of the servants to teach them their religion, it was Zedislava who helped to hear their lessons. So, although Zedislava did not go to school, she learned many things at home. They were big lessons: patience, kindness, and unselfishness — and they were not easy to learn.

While Zedislava was still quite young, she was married to an officer named Gallo. He, like her own father, commanded a fortress, the castle of Laumberg at another point on the frontier. Here she had need of all she had learned from her mother of caring for the wounded and giving food to the poor. She had even more need of those other lessons she had learned, of patience and kindness.

Gallo was a rough soldier, used to nothing but fighting. He was a good man and he loved his beautiful young wife, but he had a terrible temper and he used it much too often. Perhaps no one had ever told him it was better to be gentle and kind than to be angry and impatient. At any rate it was many years before he learned it for himself. During those years Zedislava put into practice all the patience and sweetness she had learned.

It was Zedislava's idea that Gallo have built at the gate to the castle a house where strangers could stay overnight as they passed along the road. The castle of Laumberg was on a pilgrim road over which people went each year, west to Saint James of Compostela in Spain and east to the Holy Land. These pilgrims carried clear across Europe their praises of Lady Zedislava, the gentle mistress of castle Laumberg.

One day two strangers appeared at the gates and asked to stay for the night. They were religious who wore white habits and long black cloaks. Zedislava had never seen such habits before. "You must be monks," she said, "on your way to the Holy Land."

"No, good lady," said one of the men. "We are Preaching Friars, friends of Master Dominic, the Spaniard, who is preaching in Italy. We are on our way to the north, to preach the Gospel to the Tartars."

"That would be almost certain death," she said. "Has no one told you how cruel the Tartars are?"

The friars smiled, "We are not afraid," they said. "We go to preach the Gospel of Christ, and He will take care of us. And we have a Mother in heaven who watches over us."

"Tell me more about Master Dominic and your Preaching Friars," asked Zedislava. "We are so far from everyone here we do not hear any news."

They told her about the beginnings of the Order and about its work. Zedislava was very happy when they told her she could become a Tertiary member of the Order if she wished. "I am married and have my home to look after," she said, "so I cannot go into a cloister and pray as I might want to. But if I can be a Tertiary and pray as I work, I will help the work of the Order as much as I can."

"Yes, that is the work of the Tertiaries," they told her. "And you will have a share in all the prayers and good works of everyone else in the Order."

So Zedislava became a Dominican Tertiary. She still wore her robes as lady of the castle, and the jewels and furs that Gallo liked to have her wear. She would have liked to wear the black and white habit of the Order, but it was not possible. She fasted and prayed more than ever; she was more kind and charitable than before.

All this did not mean that Zedislava did not take care of her family. She had four children to care for and teach, besides her many duties in the castle fortress. The training of the boys was mostly in the hands of their father, but her little daughter Marguerite must be taught all the things that she herself had learned. She took the little girl with her on errands of charity: to bandage the wounded, to bring food to the poor and the sick, or to visit the prisoners in the dungeons.

Lady Zedislava was very kind to her servants; she took time every day to teach them their religion. When they were sick, she herself cared for them; and she taught little Marguerite to do the same.

One day Lady Zedislava told her husband of a plan she had. "I wish to use all the money that belongs to me to build a church for the Preaching Friars right here in Bohemia. Then they can preach among our people and do much good."

"I will help you," said Gallo. "I will give you any money you need from my property. Then you will be sure to have enough."

Very soon the church was being built. People came from miles around to watch the workmen cutting the blocks of stone or raising the long beams of the roof. Sometimes the workmen would say one to another, "It's very strange about that heavy beam. It wasn't here last night. Someone must have brought it up here during the night."

Another would answer, "I think it was Lady Zedislava's prayers that moved it. And look at that pile of stones. They were down by the gate last night, and here they are this morning, all ready to use."

No one knew that Lady Zedislava herself went out in the darkness of night to move the materials where the workmen could get at them, to hurry the building of the church.

The church was hardly finished when, one sad day, Lady Zedislava died. She was very happy to go to heaven, but everyone else wept. "Who will look after us now?" said the poor. "And who will bandage our wounds?" said the sick. "A saint has left us and gone to heaven!"

Poor Gallo was heartbroken when Zedislava died. At last he saw how sweet and how good she was, and he was sorry for having been so bad tempered while she was alive. One night he was very lonely, and he sat alone in his room trying to pray. Suddenly the room filled with light. There in the glow of light was Lady Zedislava, even more beautiful than she had been on earth. Her long dress shone like some heavenly silk and she wore a crown of sparkling jewels. From her shoulders hung a long cape of purple material that was lovelier than the finest velvet.

"Do not weep, Gallo," she said. "I will always be near you because I pray for you. Only, I beg of you, take care of my poor people. They will need you, now I am gone." As he watched, the light faded and the beautiful vision was gone; but in his hands he still held a piece of the purple velvet from her long cape.

After this, Gallo was careful to put into practice all the good example Zedislava had given him. From being hot tempered and quarrelsome, he became gentle and kind. The poor and the sick did not suffer any neglect, for he took his wife's place in helping them.

The life of Blessed Zedislava can teach us more than anything else a lesson of kindness and patience. When others were angry, she was calm and gentle. Where others were cruel, she was kind. No matter what happened, she always remembered that it was the duty of a Christian to be kind, gentle, and charitable, however others may act. She did not criticize anyone who was bad tempered or unkind, but she used a very sure way of teaching them; she herself was always patient and kind. That is a lesson we can all afford to learn from this lady of long ago.

The Lawyer Who Sailed on His Cloak

IT WAS a sleepy June day in the Spain of long ago, where birds sang in the streets of Villafranca, and cats and little boys alike were too lazy even to chase them. The heavy wheels of the wine carts squeaked very slowly over the cobbled streets, for certainly a horse or a burro could not be expected to hurry on such a warm day. Even the lacemakers sat sleeping in the doorways, and children napped on the steps of the church of Saint Margaret.

On the high rock above the village of Villafranca, in the shade of the castle which crowned the rock, three boys were lying in the warm grass. From their point they could throw bits of rock down into the waters of the river just below them. They had been doing this as a good way to pass a drowsy afternoon, but now they simply lay on their backs in the grass watching the puffy clouds float by overhead. Sometimes the clouds looked like sheep, or bears, or birds, or people; it was fun to watch them twist and change in their slow rolling way until they were something else.

"I see something you don't!" said one boy. "It's a knight on horseback."

"Where, James?" asked the second boy. "I don't see it."

"Over there where the sheep was a few minutes ago," said James. "See, Raymond, that long part is the horse's head and the two little bumps are his ears. That big hump is the knight — you see, he's leaning over, and his cape is blowing in the wind."

Raymond sat up. "It does look like a knight, James. See, Rudy? Where do you suppose he's riding on such a hot day?"

Rudy grunted sleepily. "Don't know. Tournament, probably. That's where all knights go." He closed his eyes again and was almost asleep in a moment.

"Not *all* knights," said James. "I just guess I won't spend all my time at tournaments. I'm going out on missions for the king, and fight dragons, and fight. . . ."

"The Moors?" asked Raymond. "Father says they are getting very strong again. They are stealing Christians and selling them as slaves in Africa. So you'd fight the Moors."

"Of course, the Moors," James went on. "And I'm going to wear a cape of red silk, and I'm going to have a dragon on my shield. . . ."

"Too much work entirely," Rudy muttered sleepily. "You'd have to kill a dragon first, before you could have one carved on your shield."

"Well, don't you think I could kill a dragon?" asked James. "No little old dragon is going to scare me — well, not very much, anyway. I can ride pretty well now, Father says, and when I learn how to handle a sword better, and how to carry a spear. . . ."

"So you won't hit the dummy in the wrong place and make him swing around and hit you," interrupted Rudy without opening his eyes.

"Now, you look here, Rudy. It isn't any child's play to hit that dummy right so he won't swing around. You just *try* riding with a long spear in one hand and the reins in the other and go as fast as you can, and see if *you* can hit the dummy in the right place. You just try it, Mr. Rudy, and I'll bet he knocks you off your horse, too!" James sputtered.

"Mm," mumbled Rudy, "I'd rather not, thank you."

"You'll never be a knight if you don't learn how to ride with a spear!" warned James.

"Mm," said Rudy. "Not going to be a knight."

"Not going to . . ." James stopped short, his mouth opened in surprise. "Then what *are* you going to do?" he asked.

"Be a hermit," mumbled Rudy.

James looked at him in astonishment. "A hermit! Why, Rudy!"

Raymond shouted with laughter. "You look so funny, James, honestly you do! And you never will learn not to believe everything you hear! Why, if I told you I was going to be a monk, I think you'd believe that!"

"I'd know better than to believe that, I guess," said James, pouting. "Even if you are always praying — well, more than most of us, I mean. And you're smart enough. But everyone knows you are the next Count of Penafort — you couldn't be anything else but a knight like your father!"

Rudy rolled over and opened both eyes to look at Raymond. "I don't know about that," he said. "Do you mean that about being a monk, Raymond?"

Raymond smiled. "No, I don't think I'd like to be a monk, and live all my life in the same convent. I like to pray, and I like to study. But I don't know just yet what I'd like to be, or what God wants me to be."

"You could be a Knight of Calatrava and fight the Moors," said James, "or a Knight of Saint John of Jerusalem and defend Malta. They aren't just knights; they are religious too."

"We will just have to wait and see," said Raymond. "When God is ready for me to take up the work He has planned for me, He will tell me what it is, somehow. Right now, though, I am going to the cathedral school at Barcelona after Christmas."

This was news. Even Rudy sat up, and both boys looked at him. "I wish I could go with you!" said Rudy.

"Well, I don't," said James. "I don't want to spend all my

time learning Latin. Of course if you're going to be a priest. . . ."

"I didn't say I was going to be a priest," said Raymond. "I don't know whether God is calling me to that or not. But I am going to study law; and when I am older, I will know what I am going to do. By then you'll be a knight, James, with a dragon on your shield; and you'll be off fighting the Moors. And Rudy . . ."

"Yes, where will I be?" asked Rudy.

"You'll be a monk in a convent somewhere, praying for a knight and a lawyer you used to go fishing with!"

Christmas was soon past, and there was a great bustle in the house to get Raymond ready for school. It was to be his first long trip away from home, though Barcelona was not far away. All sorts of clothes must be made ready. The Count of Penafort was an important man, and his son must be dressed well for school. Dressmakers worked busily on silk jackets and hose; and made warm cloaks of fur and heavy silk, and shoes of colored leather with long pointed toes. Raymond was too busy going on last-minute hunting trips with his father, taking out his pet hawk and bringing down game birds, to watch much of what the women were doing. But, of course, the day finally came when he must be up at daybreak for the farewell Mass in the Penafort chapel; kneel for the last time in his own place under the high window, and pray for God's blessing on his new work.

Almost before he knew it the day was gone, and Penafort castle was far away. Instead of its familiar dark walls he was in a strange place with dozens of other boys. Night found him lying on a hard little straw pallet, looking up through a high window at one star shining, and wondering whether, after all, he was going to like going away to school.

He must have fallen right to sleep, for the next thing he knew he was waking with a start. Someone was pounding on the door. It couldn't be time to get up; yet someone outside the door was calling out, "Let us bless the Lord!" Raymond called a sleepy, "Thanks be to God," in answer; and tumbled out of bed to say his morning prayers. The stone floor was very cold, and the water in his pitcher had a thin coat of ice. His teeth chattering, he washed as best he could in the icy water and hurried into his clothes. He was going to see if that brother hadn't made a mistake about the time. Time to go to bed, maybe, but to get up? Never! He pushed a small desk over under the high window and climbed up to look out. Sure enough, the stars were still shining!

The chapel bell rang. Raymond jumped down and hurried down the hall, trying to fasten the last button on his cuff. "It's the middle of the night!" he said to another boy, who was straightening his collar.

"Sh!" said the boy. "Can't talk until after breakfast!"

There were three Masses, and Raymond looked enviously at the boys who served them. They looked so very important, and they seemed to know exactly what to do and when to do it. The bell rang for the *Sanctus.* "Holy, holy, holy!" For a moment Raymond was homesick; but then he thought, "We are always near our dear ones when we are at Mass. Mass is always the same."

With the stars still twinkling through the open arches of the building, he hurried down the cloister walk with the other boys for breakfast. No more of the fruits and fine meats he had enjoyed at home; instead, Raymond ate his small loaf of brown bread and drank his cup of milk in silence, listening to the tall boy who stood at the center of the room reading from a huge book about the life of a saint. It was all in Latin, but Raymond understood most of it. The life of Saint Anthony the Hermit it was today. He thought of Rudy and kept from smiling just in time. It must be very hard, he thought, to go away out in the desert to live, with only the stars for company and almost nothing to eat. Well, it wasn't much easier, he decided, getting up and starting school so early in the morning!

Morning lecture started at six o'clock. The classroom was very cold and dark except for the candles around the master's desk. Raymond sat cross-legged on a bundle of straw on the hard stone floor and tried to keep his eyes open. He saw the other boys writing in their copybooks, so he did the same, for he knew he would have to study from his own notes afterward. The lessons were all in Latin, too, and he followed the best he could. After it was all over, he looked at the notes in his copybook. Most of the writing, he was sorry to say, was pretty bad. Mother would shake her head over that. And here, where the writing ran clear off the page, was where he had fallen asleep.

After the morning lesson and before the master's noon lecture, there was choir practice. This was easy, for always at home Raymond had loved to sing. "I will lift up mine eyes to the mountains," sang the boys. Suddenly before Raymond's eyes his own mountains rose up, white and blue against the gray stones of the church. There was lovely Montserrat where the shrine of our Lady was; nearer, snowy Tibidabo from which, so people said, the devil had showed our Lord the kingdoms of the world. And before Raymond could stop them, two big round tears spilled over the edge of his lashes and went rolling over his round cheeks and down his lace collar to the front of his jacket!

Before two more could follow, Raymond felt a sharp punch in the ribs. It was Frederick, one of the older boys. "You'll get used to it," he whispered, "and for goodness sake, *sing!* Brother John is looking at you. Want him to scold you?" And Raymond sang.

Raymond was not long in getting used to the cathedral school. Soon he, too, was serving two and three Masses each morning, and saying the Office in choir with the older

[62]

boys and the priests of the cathedral. He learned to like the boys in his class, and they liked him. He was good at running and wrestling and jumping, and all the games boys like. There was only one thing they knew Raymond wouldn't do — and that was to join in telling bad stories or using bad language. More than one of them had taken a good thrashing from Raymond for using the Holy Name carelessly in his hearing, so they were careful what they said.

There was no vacation for the cathedral boys to spend at home. School kept open all year round, except for the holidays which were really the holydays of the Church. Raymond often thought how nice it was to belong to the Communion of the Saints; for it was just like having a lot of brothers and sisters, and celebrating all their birthdays.

In the spring, after Easter, were the Rogation Days. Raymond was proud to be an acolyte and carry a torch beside the priest as he went slowly around the garden chanting the Litany of the Saints while all the people answered. That, one of the older boys told him, was to bless the garden and pray that God would give them a good harvest; and protect them from earthquake, fire, and the Moors. Rogation Days were great holidays for the cathedral boys; for they meant three days free from classes and, after the processions, picnics and fun.

When the leaves turned yellow and the birds began to go south the older boys began talking about the Christmas season. Before then would be the gay feast of Saints Clement and Catherine, when children would dress in old clothes and go from house to house begging apples "tricks or treat." But the greatest of all the year's feasts was Christmas. "That's when we have the boy bishop," Frederick said one day to a group of the younger boys.

"Boy bishop?" asked Raymond. "Why, what does he do?"

"Oh, it's great fun," said John, another of the older boys. "It all begins on the eve of Saint Nicholas — December 5, you know — and it lasts all the children's season until Holy Innocents Day on the 28."

"We'll begin practicing soon," said Frederick. "You see, the boy who behaves the best during the year is chosen to be bishop, and others are chosen for his helpers. Then they are measured for their robes so the tailor can make their clothes. They have to practice going up and down from the bishop's throne and giving the blessing and preaching. There's a lot to learn."

"What happens first?" Raymond wanted to know. "For the feast, I mean?"

"The boy is chosen to be bishop," said John. "He is dressed up like a bishop for Vespers on Saint Nicholas' Eve. Then at the *Magnificat* of Vespers — that's the hymn, I suppose you know — when they come to the verse, 'He hath put down the mighty from their thrones and hath exalted the humble . . .' then the real bishop gets up and comes down from his throne; and the boy bishop goes up in his place."

"Then he preaches at the High Mass on Saint Nicholas' Day," Frederick went on. "In the afternoon he rides a white horse through the streets and blesses all the people. Then he goes to a banquet at the real bishop's house, and all his helpers get to go with him. My brother James went one year, and you should hear him tell about that banquet!"

"But the real bishop?" asked Raymond. "What happens to him all this time?"

"He's just an altar boy," said Frederick. "I wish I'd been here the year he dropped the censer in the aisle. It must have been awfully funny."

"My, but I wish Christmas would hurry up and get here!" said one of the other little boys. "How long is it, Raymond, until Christmas?"

Christmases came and went and Raymond, like all the boys, looked forward with joy to each one. Only now Raymond was one of the older boys helping to teach the smaller boys who came to the cathedral school. Perhaps he was a boy bishop himself for one of the many Christmas seasons there at Barcelona; but no one thought to write it down whether he was or not, so we couldn't say for sure. But he was a good student, and everyone knew how often he went to Holy Communion, and how devout he was in serving Mass. They knew, too, how clean his conversation was, and they must have known that his heart was very pure. He would have made a good boy bishop. Only, as we say, no one wrote down some of the things we would most like to know.

When he was twenty, Raymond had finished all that the schools at Barcelona could teach him; and after teaching a few years there himself, he set out for Bologna in Italy to study law.

Everyone was sorry to see him go; but one day in the early spring when all the fruit trees around Barcelona were in bloom, Master Raymond set out on foot for Italy. Perhaps some of his boys walked a few miles with him as he left the towers of Barcelona behind him, and set out on the ancient Roman road that led off into the hills. That road was the one taken by the Apostle Saint James, so the legends said, when he came into Spain long ago to preach the Gospel. Now as Raymond walked along it, he must have wondered what God had planned for him. As yet he did not know, but his mind was well trained and his heart was pure; he would be ready whenever the Lord should call him.

Raymond worked hard at the University of Bologna. While he taught others, he still studied to learn as much as he could. Soon there was no more famous man in Bologna than the Doctor of Church Law, Raymond of Penafort. He taught on and on and probably thought he would spend the rest of his life teaching when, one day, strangers came to Bologna; and they made all the difference in the world to Raymond.

It was the students who first told Master Raymond about those strange men in black and white — Friars Preachers, they called themselves. And the students were so excited about them that they did not even stop to knock at Master Raymond's door. "Master Raymond! Master Raymond!" they cried, rushing in. "They . . . they . . . "

"Who?" asked Master Raymond with a smile. "And what have they done?"

"Please, Sir — it's Master Moneta — he's gone with the Preachers, Sir!"

"Oh, certainly not Master Moneta!" exclaimed Raymond. "Why he wouldn't even go to hear the Friars preach for fear he would become one of them!"

"He's done it," the students went on. "His students wanted him to hear a certain Master Reginald, a Frenchman who fairly kidnaps their souls while they listen to him. He tried to get out of it, but they made him go; only he insisted on going to Mass first. He stayed for three Masses in the hope that Master Reginald would be through preaching by the time they reached him — but he wasn't. And now, Master Moneta has gone with them himself!"

"Master Moneta!" said Raymond. "And only a little while ago it was Master Roland, another teacher; and Claro, the famous lawyer!"

"All the world is gone after the Friars; they are such holy men!" cried a student. "Dominic, the founder — he is a Spaniard like yourself, Master Raymond — is to visit here soon; and perhaps you will see him then."

"I hope I shall," said Raymond.

Raymond did indeed meet Dominic, though not in Bologna. They met as Raymond was on his way back to Barcelona to teach. Raymond could never forget the tall quiet man with the kind eyes. In fact, he found himself thinking more and more about the saintly Dominic, and about the Preaching Friars who were already scattering all over the known world. So one Good Friday he went to the convent of the Friars in Barcelona and asked to be taken into their Order.

All Barcelona was talking over this news — Master Raymond, the great lawyer, had gone to the Preaching Friars! He was wearing a poor habit of white wool, like the poorest pilgrim — he who was the Count of Penafort and the greatest lawyer in Spain!

Father Raymond did not mind being poor. He was happy in serving God, and so humble that no one could have guessed that he had been such an important man. He had always loved to study the Bible — in fact, he knew a great deal of it by heart — and he was happy in his new life of prayer and study. He had already been ordained a priest when he entered the Order, but he was as humble as the youngest novice in the house.

Soon the pope found out that a famous lawyer had entered the Order of Friars Preachers. He gave to Father Raymond a very hard piece of work to do. This was to write down all the Church laws into one book. He did this so well that the pope gave him other work to do.

All this time, Father Raymond could not forget what all Spaniards watched with fear and sorrow — the Moors coming over from Africa and laying waste to Christian Spain. The Moors had taken thousands of Christians prisoners and carried them off to Africa to sell as slaves. Here they lived in terror; and many, to escape death, denied their faith and became Mohammedans. Christian knights fought and died to stop this dreadful sale of Christians, but no one could stop it. Sometimes the Moors would hold for a high ransom any prisoner they thought might have the money

The Christ Child appears to Saint Raymond of Penafort during Mass.

to pay for freedom, but the poorer captives suffered dreadful things. Father Raymond and his friend, Father Peter Nolasco, often talked about this sad state of affairs.

"There should be knights whose lifework it would be to ransom captives," said Father Raymond: "just as it is our work to preach truth, and the work of the Knights of Saint John to defend the Holy Sepulcher. There should be an order that will pay the Moors what they ask, and free all the captives they can. If it must be, they should be ready to sell themselves into slavery to free any captives they cannot free any other way."

"We will need the king to help us, and the pope to give us his blessing; and men who are willing to begin such an order," said his friend.

At first the king was not too pleased with the idea. "There are many religious orders now," he said. "Can't one of those take care of this work?"

But the next night the king was awakened by a vision in which our Lady appeared, telling him to give his help to the new order. The same night, our Lady also appeared to both Father Raymond and Father Peter. They did not wait any longer, but went ahead with the plans. One day not long after that, thirteen brave men knelt at the altar of the cathedral and were made the first members of the new Order of Our Lady of Mercy. The two priests were there to give them their special blessing; and, as both of them were saints, it is not surprising that their prayers were answered.

Many people thought Father Raymond was a saint, even when he was living. One who thought so was a Dominican brother whose mind was troubled with terrible thoughts. "I know they are not sins as long as I do not want them there in my mind," he said over and over again to himself. "But I am so afraid that sometime I will slip and begin enjoying them. How I wish I could be rid of such awful

He sailed on his cloak.

thoughts, and think good things." Thinking these things, he went in to serve Father Raymond's Mass. Kneeling on the altar steps, he watched the holy man saying Mass. Father Raymond did not seem to know he was there at all, or to care about anything else in the world but the sacrifice of the Mass. The brother rang the bell for the consecration and watched the holy priest lift up the sacred Host at the elevation. Then he almost cried aloud in surprise; for instead of the white Host, Father Raymond seemed to be holding in his hands a beautiful child all shining with light! There was no use to ask who the beautiful child was — it was the Babe of Bethlehem! And from that hour the brother had no more trouble with his thoughts.

The miracle that boys and girls all like best in the life of Saint Raymond — for we call him that now, instead of Father Raymond — is that of his trip across the water on his mantle. It happened this way:

The King of Spain, who was very fond of Father Raymond, ordered him to come to the palace and be his adviser. Father Raymond would much rather have stayed at home in his convent than to go into the noisy and wicked court; but he was told to go, and go he did — to an island where the court was at the time. But he soon found out that the king had not much intention of being good; and was, in fact, giving very bad example to his people. Father Raymond told the king he must either mend his ways or look for another adviser. The king only laughed.

"Pooh!" said the king. "He can't tell me what to do! I'll show him!" So he called all the captains of his navy together and told them that no one should dare to take Father Raymond home on any ship. "There!" said the king with a wicked chuckle. "If he wants to get home, he will have to swim; and it's a hundred and sixty miles!"

Father Raymond was as good as his word. He hadn't much to pack so it didn't take him long, and in no time at all he was down on the dock ready to go. But it was very strange, he thought, none of the ship captains could be seen anywhere; and no one seemed to want to talk to him. He soon found out why. "We're sorry, Father, but we don't dare to take you back to Spain. It's the king's orders."

"I guess you will just have to stay with us," said one of the captains. And they all went back to their ships.

A few minutes later a sailor's shout brought them all on deck again. "Hi! Come back here! You'll drown yourself!" cried the excited man. For there was Father Raymond very calmly sailing off across the water on his cloak! One corner of it he had fastened to his staff, and the wind was skimming him along over the waves as smoothly as though he were sailing on clear ice!

Father Raymond lived to be a hundred years old, so, many more exciting things happened to him. The Order of Our Lady of Mercy, which he helped to start, grew and did a great deal of good. His law books were used all over Europe. Kings and popes called on him for advice on many things. For some time he was Master General of the Friars and so had to travel all over Europe on foot to visit the houses of his Order. The little boy playing around his father's castle long ago could never have imagined that he would do so much in one lifetime.

Finally, even his long hundred years were past, and God called him to heaven. So many people had come to depend on Father Raymond for their hard thinking, that they hardly knew what to do without him. They knew, though, that as he had been so willing to help anyone on earth, he would still help them from heaven. Especially would he be anxious to help boys and girls to practice the virtues that were so great in him: purity of thought, word, and action; obedience; and humility.

Little Sister Princess

"MARGUERITE! Marguerite! Little Sister Princess!" Helene, who had gathered her long skirts up to the knee so it would be easier to run, went clattering down the hall calling for her friend. A sister's voice stopped her.

"My Lady Helene," said the sister, "is that the way your mother, the countess, would like her daughter to go down a hall? Or our Lady Mother, Queen of Heaven?"

Helene let her skirts down and dropped a curtsy. "No, Reverend Mother," she said. "I'm sorry. I wanted Marguerite, and I forgot."

"Princess Marguerite is in chapel, I think," said the sister. "Now try to walk down the hall like a lady, if you please."

Helene was walking down the hall, very much like a lady, when the chapel door at the end of the hall opened. A small figure dressed in black and white came out; and Helene hurried her steps, almost tripping over her long skirt. Little Sister Princess was only five, and so small that she looked like a big doll dressed in a sister's habit.

"I'm so glad you're through praying for a while," Helene said breathlessly. "We want you to play a guessing game. You're always so good at guessing what the other side is acting out."

Marguerite did not answer until they were outside the door; then she turned to her friend with a happy smile. "You know, Helene," she said, "I asked Sister Elizabeth

She remembered the day Marguerite had come
to the convent to live.

again this morning if she would let me go in for all the Office with the sisters, and she said I might. Now I can learn the rest of it. I'm so happy!"

"What do you want to learn all that Office for?" asked Helene. "You won't be staying here as a sister when you're older — you know you won't!"

"Oh, yes I will!" said Marguerite. "Why, I was promised to God, years ago. I belong to Him. That's why the sisters let me wear the habit since I was three years old. Of course I'll stay here!"

"But Marguerite — you're the Crown Princess of Hungary! You'll sit on a throne some day!"

"I hope so," said Marguerite, "in heaven."

Helene shook her head. She remembered the day Marguerite had come to the convent to live. The king and queen had brought her. Helene, with the other little girls who lived with the sisters, had hidden at the bottom of the staircase to see the little princess. Everyone knew the story of the princess; of how the Tartars had come riding into Hungary, burning and killing; of the king and queen riding for days to get away from them and finally hiding on a small island; of their promise that Marguerite should be given to God if they were saved; and of the Tartars leaving them in peace to go back to their own country. Yes, everyone knew that the princess had many reasons to stay at the convent of Vesprem. But still, she *was* a princess, and some day her father might want to make a royal marriage for her.

When Marguerite was seven, that very question came up. Marriages were made very early in those days; and a young prince, who had heard that Marguerite was both good and beautiful, asked for her hand in marriage. The King of Hungary came to see his daughter about it. "I'm sorry, Father, to disappoint you," she said to him; "but I belong here with the sisters. I belong to Jesus."

"But Marguerite," said her father; "your mother and I did promise you to God if you wanted to be a sister. We put you here in the convent when you were very tiny so you could learn to read and write and embroider, and to learn all the things that a princess should know. But we did not mean that you had to stay here as a sister if you didn't want to when you were older."

"But I do want to," said Marguerite. "I am very happy."

"Very well," said the king. "Stay, and be happy."

The king had built for Marguerite a new convent on an island in the Danube River near Budapest. This little island was called "The Blessed Virgin's Isle" for many years; but, because of Sister Marguerite, it was later called "Isle of Marguerite." Many sisters lived there and were very happy to live with their princess, for she was both good and kind.

When Marguerite was twelve, a visitor came to the little island. This was Father Humbert, a Friar Preacher who had charge of the Order at that time. "I would like to see Sister Marguerite," he said. "I have heard that she is very holy."

The sister who answered the door was very happy to tell him that what he heard was true. "She has been a saint, I'm sure, since she was a baby. Why, when she was only four years old, she was praying and doing penances that many older people would be afraid to try. She loves our Lord so much that she does not care how much He asks her to suffer."

Sister Marguerite was very happy to see Father Humbert. "Now I can make my vows," she said. "Sister told me I would have to wait until you came. Now you are here, so I need not wait any longer."

"Suppose that your father wanted to make a royal marriage for you?" asked Father Humbert. "Wouldn't you be happier as queen of a castle than as a sister?"

Sister Marguerite shook her head. "No, Father, I am happy here, with Jesus in the Blessed Sacrament and with my sisters. Please let me make my vows, so I can belong to Jesus forever."

One day soon after this, the king and queen were invited to the convent to hear Sister Marguerite make her promise to Jesus that she would love and serve Him only. The princess knelt in front of Father Humbert and placed her hand on the big rule book which he held. She made her vows, the promises which all sisters make, of poverty, chastity, and obedience. "Now," she thought to herself, "I belong to Jesus; all of me: my thoughts, my words, my actions. I belong to Him forever. Now no one will bother me any more about a royal marriage. I am vowed to the King of kings."

But she was wrong. Word went around in all the courts that there was not a princess so fair and so good as Marguerite. When she was eighteen, the King of Bohemia came asking for her hand.

"She cannot marry you or anyone else," said her father, "because she has taken her vows. She belongs to God."

"I will get the pope's permission," begged the King of Bohemia. "He can free her from her promises."

Once more her father tried to arrange a marriage for Marguerite, and again she refused. "Once and for all," she said, "I belong to God." So the King of Bohemia had to go home disappointed. The Princess of Hungary was interested only in the King of heaven.

No one would know that Sister Marguerite was a princess as she went about her work with the other sisters. She took her turn in sweeping, washing, and waiting table; and she did everything so cheerfully that others liked to work with her. Carrying wood and water, washing dishes, and scrubbing the floors was hard work even for those who were healthy. It was doubly hard for a princess who had never been very strong. When she was tired or ill, or the work was heavy for her, she did not complain or leave the work for someone else to do. She went right ahead and did her work, smiling.

It was Sister Marguerite's cheerfulness and kindness that made her so welcome in the sickroom. If heads were aching or fevers were high, it was always Sister Marguerite who was sent to help the sick person. She always knew what to say and do to make the patient comfortable.

For all her busy hours about the convent and the sickroom, Sister Marguerite did not ever let her work stop her prayer. Her special devotions were to the Holy Name of Jesus, to the Holy Cross, and to our Lady whom she called "Our Sweet Hope." On the day before Christmas, she would say the "Our Father" a thousand times; on the eve of any feast of our Lady, the "Hail Mary" a thousand times. Since she knew she could never visit the holy places of Rome and Jerusalem, she counted up the miles that lay between Hungary and those shrines. When she wanted to go on a visit to one of them, she would say a "Hail Mary" for each mile that it would take to get there.

When anyone would speak of Sister Marguerite as a princess, or talk about the wealth of her family, she would talk instead about its saints. There had been several saints in her family; of whom Saint Stephen, king, and Saint Elizabeth of Hungary are the ones we remember best today. Sister Marguerite never tired of reading about these holy people, of telling others about them, and of trying to imitate them.

Sometimes when Sister Marguerite was praying, she would be raised in the air, or would seem to be asleep. That was because she was praying so hard she forgot all about the world around her and thought only of Jesus.

Sister Marguerite went to heaven while she was still quite young. Ten days before her death, she told her sisters she was going to heaven soon. On the very day she had told them she would die, she did so.

[78]

After the death of the holy sister, many people came to her tomb to pray for her help. No less than two hundred miracles took place near her tomb. Even today, Saint Margaret of Hungary is called upon when there is danger of flood, because she stopped the Danube from flooding several times. We can pray to her, not only when there is danger of floods or drowning, but any time, that she will help us to be prayerful and humble. We may never be offered an earthly throne, as she was, but we do wish to share with her the reward of heaven.

A Book With Golden Pages

"FATHER said *he* didn't have time to tell me a story about Saint James, and I thought maybe *you* would?" The little boy looked up hopefully at his mother.

"I'm sorry James I'm busy now, too," said his mother. "Maybe you could ask your Aunt Agnes."

James went obediently to find Aunt Agnes, but she was busy too. So were his uncle and the gardner. Finally he hunted out an old man who begged at one of the city gates. "Do *you* know the story of Saint James so you could tell it to me?" he asked.

The old man shook his head. "I'm afraid I don't," he said. "Why?"

"I want somebody to tell me a story," said James, sitting down beside the beggar, "and nobody has time. Everybody is too busy."

"Can't you read a story yourself?" asked the beggar. "You look like a smart boy."

"Of course, I can read," said James. "But I want a story about Saint James — *my* Saint James. And we don't have a book with that story in it."

"That's too bad," said the old man.

"Believe me," said James, "when I grow up I'm going to *write* a book with stories in it about the saints. Then anybody can read it. There won't be just one book in town so that everybody has to go to that one place and listen to someone read."

"That sounds like a good idea," encouraged the old man.

James was quiet for a minute; then he had a new thought. "If you don't know any stories about Saint James, do you know any about Saint Peter?"

"No," said the old man. "At least not very much about him."

"Or Saint John?" asked James, adding to himself, "I know most of them already, but I like to hear people tell them over again."

"No," said the beggar, "I couldn't tell you about Saint John either."

"Do you know anything about Saint Dominic, then?" asked James. "He died just a few years ago. I should think you would know something about him."

The old man shook his head.

"Don't *you* know *any* stories about saints?" asked the little boy.

"I knew them, long ago," the old man said, "but one forgets."

"Well, then I guess I had better tell *you* one," said James. "How would you like a story about Saint Dominic and his Dominican Friars?"

The beggar nodded, so he began eagerly, "You see, the Master Dominic was a very holy man. He worked many miracles. The one I like best is about the angels and the bread. This one day the brothers had nothing to eat, so two of them went out to beg for bread. Someone gave them a small loaf, and they were coming home with it when they met a poor man; so, of course, they gave it to him. When they came in with nothing at all, Saint Dominic told them to ring the bell for dinner anyway. They rang it; and everybody came in, said grace, and sat down. But there wasn't anything on the table to eat. All of a sudden there were two beautiful angels standing there, with their arms full of bread. They passed it around to the brothers and there was

Blessed James of Voragine writes a book with golden pages.

enough for everybody. There was even some left over. Master Dominic could perform miracles, you see, because he was a friend of God. He was a saint. The Friars say that the Holy Father in Rome canonized him just four years ago, so that all the world will know he is a saint."

"That was a fine story," said the beggar. "I hope you do write that book some day."

James was not the only little boy of his time who wished he could get storybooks to read. It was true enough, there were pictures of the saints on the walls of the churches, and those who could not read could tell from these pictures what the story was about. Then at the feasts of the different saints, sermons were preached about them, and the stories of their lives would be told. But for James, who would have liked to hear their legends three or four times a day instead of just once a year, that was not enough.

Books at that time were costly and hard to get. The churches and convents, and some few of the wealthy homes, had libraries; but no one else did. This may seem strange to boys and girls of today who have so many books of their own, but seven hundred years ago there were no presses to print the books. Each had to be made by hand. Patient monks, working at a book, sometimes spent forty years in making one copy. The pages of books were made of sheepskin, and every letter of every word was printed in by hand. Capital letters were painted with gold and bright colors. Sometimes a small picture was painted in the capital, and dragons or other queer little animals were painted here and there on the page. When finished, a page of one of those old books was so beautiful that people would come from miles around to see it. When the whole book was finished it was not only big and heavy, but also valuable. For this reason the Bibles and hymn books were often chained to the stands which held them. The priest or someone else usually read the stories to the people, because many of them could not read for themselves. Naturally, as far as boys were concerned, people felt it was just as well if they kept their hands off such precious books!

James had a long way to go before he was to see his dream come true. First he studied a great deal; and that meant, of course, that he studied in Latin. Then one day he knocked at the door of the Preaching Friars and asked to be admitted to their Order. They were very glad to accept him, and he was given the habit. After he had made his studies, he was ordained to the priesthood and began his real work.

James became first of all a famous preacher. "If I preach in Latin, some people will understand me and be helped by the sermon," he said. "But if I preach in Italian, they will all understand." So he preached in Italian, and thousands who flocked to hear him were led by his sermons to live a better life.

The feast days of the saints were kept with great joy at that time. There would be music and processions and a High Mass, and a sermon about the life of the saint. Very often James was asked to give the sermon. He wrote down the stories of the saints when he was getting ready to preach. Soon he had a whole book full of stories of the saints. Other priests heard about this book of sermons and sent scribes to copy the book for them. Preaching Friars going to other parts of Italy took copies with them. Wherever they went, people liked the stories and insisted on having them told over and over again.

James did not invent the stories of the saints which he put in his book. He wrote down all that was really known and written about them, all that the Church believed about them, and most of the legends that had been told from person to person down through the years. Although James called his book *Legends of the Saints,* the book was soon so loved that people changed its name to *The Golden Legend.*

Scribes came from France, Spain, Germany, and other countries to copy the wonderful book into their own language.

Writing *The Golden Legend* and translating the Bible into Italian, as James did, would seem to us enough for one man to do. But James became famous for still another reason. He was made bishop of a part of Italy that had been at war for years. The two armies had all but torn the land to pieces. Each was sure the other was wrong, and no one would give in. Even the pope had tried to make peace, and no one would listen to him. So when James was given the task of making peace between the armies and building up the cities they had ruined, it was almost too much to expect that he would succeed, but he did.

The troops laid down their arms and turned in together to build up the country. Word went all over Italy that Bishop James, the Preaching Friar, had made peace. People began calling him "The Peacemaker," and the pope sent him to settle several quarrels. By his prayers and his preaching he settled all of them. It was because of his work as a peacemaker that he was enrolled among the blesseds of the Church.

But it is for his stories of the saints that we remember him best today. Blessed James of Voragine, safe in heaven among the saints he so loved to write about, would teach us to love and honor the saints. More than that, he would tell us to try to imitate them. Every Catholic boy and girl has a patron saint to help him to win heaven. Today any child can get books to read about the saints, for since the days of *The Golden Legend* thousands of books have been printed. How much do *you* know of your patron saint, and how often do you try to imitate him in his sanctity?

The Heavenly Gardener

"IT'S a flower," said the little girl.

"It's a weed," answered her brother.

"Well, it's pretty and I like it," said she. "Even if it is a weed, I like it. I'm going to take it to Brother Albert, and maybe he could tell us a story about it." She picked the flower and took it carefully in both hands.

"Did I hear someone saying my name?" asked Albert, coming down the garden path. He set down a shovel and a basket of young plants. "Was it you, Marie?" he asked.

"Yes, Brother, we were talking about this flower," she said. "George says it's a weed, and I say it's a flower. And I knew you'd be able to tell us a story about it."

"I thought it would be a story you wanted," said Albert, taking the flower into his own hands. "That's a morning-glory, Marie, but sometimes people call it 'Traveler's Joy' or 'The Friar's Journey.'"

"Why, Brother Albert?" they asked together. "Won't you tell us?"

"It's a very strange story," said Albert, sitting down on a big stone as they sat down in the grass. "And it's about the holy Master Dominic. Do you know who he was?"

"I do," said George. "He preached the rosary, and he started the Friars of Mary."

"That's right," said Albert. "And this story is about the time he was going from one city to another to preach, and he lost his way. He met a man on the road and asked him how to get to the next town. Now, this man was a heretic and he didn't like the Preaching Friars. So he said yes, he knew the way. All he wanted to do was to give the holy man trouble; but Dominic didn't know that, so he thanked the heretic and went along with him. Master Dominic used to take off his shoes when he left the cities, and walk in his bare feet for penance; and the heretic had noticed this. So he led him up hill and down dale, over the rockiest paths he knew. There were briars to sting the Friar's feet, and thorns and rocks to cut them. But Dominic did not seem to care. The more the thorns hurt him, the more he would smile, because he had something to suffer for our Lord. Finally they reached the top of a rocky, thorny path that had bruised them at every step. And instead of complaining, Dominic began to sing! The heretic saw how wicked he had been to make the good man suffer so. He knelt down and begged Dominic's pardon. Then he showed him the right path; and as they went on, they sang together. And people do say that the morning-glory grew wherever Dominic walked that day. The white of its petals is the white of his habit, and the little red spots in the center are the drops of blood where the thorns hurt him. At least, that's what the legends say."

"That's a lovely story, Brother Albert," said Marie.

By this time, other children had joined the group. They knew that when Brother Albert put down his spade, they might ask him for a story; and they gladly left their play to listen. So they begged, "Tell us another!"

"Tell us one about Christmas!" begged one child.

"Yes, please, Brother Albert," said Marie. "You know, you never finished the one about the mistletoe."

"Oh, yes, the mistletoe," he said. "It's hardly a good time to tell it now, with spring flowers in the garden."

"Tell it anyway!" begged one child. "Please!"

Blessed Albert of Bergamo teaches the little children.

"Well, then," said Albert. "All this happened a long, long time ago when our dear Lord was on earth. How long ago was that, George?"

"More than 1250 years ago," said George proudly.

"Just so," said Albert. "And it all happened, this story about the mistletoe I mean, one day when the flowers in the forest were talking. For our Lady often walked there in the woods, with the little Jesus asleep in her arms. And the flowers were very proud of this — which is foolish, my children, oh, very foolish. The rose put up her beautiful head and told the others how much our Lady liked roses. 'They call her Mystical Rose,' said the rose, 'so I'm sure we must be her favorite flower.' 'No,' said the lily, 'for she is also called Lily of Israel. She must like the lilies best.' Then the other flowers started in to boast, too. They had kept this up for quite a while when one of them spied a little branch of mistletoe, high on a branch over the pathway. 'Humph!' said the proud little flower, 'I'm certainly glad I'm not the mistletoe. No flowers at all, poor homely thing!' But the mistletoe said nothing. She was too humble to worry about what people thought of her. But our Lady knew all about the proud little flowers, so what do you think she did? That day, when she came walking through the forest, with the little Jesus asleep in her arms, she stopped under the branch where the mistletoe hung. She raised her head, and three pearls from her crown caught in the mistletoe branch. 'Keep them as a gift from me,' she said to the little plant, 'and always be happy, for I love you too.' So, to this day, children, the mistletoe has no flowers — but everyone knows that the little white berries it wears are the pearls from our Lady's crown."

"That one was even nicer, Brother Albert," said George, "and thank you for telling us."

"Do you suppose our Lady scolded the other flowers, because they were so proud?" asked little Joseph.

"Oh, I don't think so," said Marie, quickly. "Do you, Brother Albert? Because our Lady loves flowers."

"Yes, our Lady loves the flowers," said Albert. "I think sometimes God must have made the flowers just for His Mother. Of course, though, they are like everything else in this beautiful world, made to teach us to love God." He leaned over to pick a lovely iris that grew beside the rock, and held it up for them to see.

"You see, little one, how carefully God makes the flowers," said Albert. "Look at this lovely iris. It has a dress of purple velvet, and a ruffle of gold lace, and a stem of green silk. You could not find anywhere in the world any cloth so lovely as this little flower is wearing. Our weavers work day and night, and our dyers mix their finest colors to make cloth beautiful, and they cannot make anything so lovely as this. And how long will this flower live, Marie?"

"Just a little while," answered Marie. "Maybe only a few days."

"And how long will your soul live, my child?" he asked.

"Forever," she said.

"So you see, my dear, how very, very lovely your soul must be. He makes flowers so beautiful, and they will live only a few days. Your soul He makes to live forever. How beautiful it must be, and how terrible to soil it by sin!"

"Tell us another story, Brother Albert," begged the little boy.

"I'm afraid I haven't time today, my dears," he said. "I must get to work. But some other time I will tell you about the forget-me-not, which is so blue that we call it 'Our Lady's Eyes,' and the little white flower, 'Our Lady's Lace.' Oh, there are hundreds of flowers named for our Lady; and they all have stories, if we only had time for them all."

"Who told you all the stories about the flowers, Brother Albert?" asked Marie.

Albert smiled. "My father did," he said. "When I was a

little boy — oh, not any bigger than you are, George — I used to be out in the fields helping my father, and he would tell me about God and the beautiful things in the world around us. When you live out in the country, there is much to remind you of God. In the daytime there are green fields, and flowers, and birds, and growing things to care for; and you think how God made all these things to make us think of heaven. At night there are the stars to remind you that God never sleeps, but watches over us always."

"Did you always live in the country?" asked George.

"For many years," said Albert. "Now, when I live in the city where the Dominican fathers have their convent, they let me keep their gardens for them."

Albert might have told the children, too, that when he was only seven he had fasted and prayed much, and had given all his money to the poor. But perhaps they already knew it, for everyone in town was sure that Albert was a saint. They called him "Brother Albert" although he was a Tertiary, and did not live in the house with the fathers. He worked hard and gave away his money as fast as he earned it. That was indeed reason for people to talk.

Albert had been married as a young man to a woman who scolded and nagged at him because of his prayers and penances. But because he was so patient and kind, she had stopped scolding, and she became very holy herself before she died.

But that had been many years ago; and since then Albert had traveled far. He had been a pilgrim for several years, visiting the most famous shrines in the world. He went eight times to the shrine of Saint James at Compostella, nine times to Rome, and once to the Holy Land. On all these journeys he had walked, as a pilgrim should, and begged his food wherever he happened to be.

A strange little story is told of how Albert cut the grain.

[91]

While on his trips to the shrines, Albert stopped to work for a while in the fields. It was harvest time, and there were many other workers on the same farm. At night, when they would bring in their grain to be weighed, Albert always had twice as much as anyone else.

"There is something wrong here," the men said one to another. "We'll have to see how he does it."

"I'll watch him tomorrow," said one of the men. So he did. When he came back at night to report, he was shaking his head. "I can't understand it," he said. "I look here, and he is working here; I look there, he is working there. There are *two* of him. He isn't just one man; he's two men!"

The other workers made great fun of him. "You certainly must have stood too long in the hot sun," they said. "*Two* of him! Humph! Tomorrow, we will watch for ourselves."

But the next day there were two Alberts again. When the time came to weigh the grain, there was only one; but he had twice as much grain, so he was given double pay. This he took out and gave to the poor.

"I will take good care that he does not earn so much tomorrow," said one man. "Just leave it to me." So he stayed up most of the night planting pieces of iron among the grain where Albert would be cutting the next day. "There now," he said. "As soon as his blade touches those, it will be dulled. He will have to spend the whole day sharpening his blade."

In the meantime, Albert was in his little room, saying his rosary. He did not know that other people were puzzled about him. He knew, of course, that it was his guardian angel helping him to cut the grain. But why should anyone care, as long as he gave the money to the poor?

The next day the other workers were on hand early to see the fun. But there was no fun. For Albert's blade cut the grain as though it were butter; and the men stood terrified to see the two good workers cutting right through the iron, right along with the grain!

Albert worked for a long time to earn money enough to build a hospital. In this, poor pilgrims who had nowhere to go when they were sick or old, could be cared for as long as they needed care. Albert kept the fathers' garden, prayed his rosary, and told the children stories when he had the time. His cheerfulness and his humility made everyone love him.

One day Albert became suddenly ill. He knew he was going to die, and he sent for the priest. Because the priest was delayed, a dove came to Albert's room, bringing him Holy Communion while there was still time.

Blessed Albert of Bergamo, the humble pilgrim, gardener, and Tertiary, can teach us that one sure way to be a saint is to be humble and kind. What our work might be does not matter at all. God will not ask us what work we have done, but He will ask how well we did it. If we can tell Him that we have worked as hard as the humble gardner of Bergamo, then surely we will enjoy with him the reward of eternity.

Rich Little Poor Girl

IF THERE was anything Catherine hated, it was washing dishes. Not that she minded the work, but she was sure that in Racconigi, perhaps in all Italy, there was not another little girl with such slippery fingers. Hardly a week went by that she didn't break a dish — and that was dreadful when there was no money to buy more.

Crash! It had happened again. Catherine groaned and gathered up the pieces in her apron. She heard the clack-clack-clack of the loom slow down and stop, and her mother's voice call from inside the house, "Catherine! Come here to me!"

The little girl went into the room where her mother had been weaving at the big loom. "I'm sorry, Mother," she said. "Truly I am. I am very clumsy."

"I should say you are clumsy!" scolded the mother. "Pretty soon we won't have a dish left in the house. If you would stop your praying and pay attention to what you are doing, you might not be forever breaking things."

Catherine went back to the porch feeling very sad. It wasn't any use trying to explain to her mother that it wasn't the prayers that made her break the dishes. And she could not help thinking of Jesus all the time, now that she had seen Him and knew how beautiful He is. So she said over again the little prayer she always said when she needed His help — "Jesus, our hope" — and went back, with a sigh, to the dishes.

She remembered the first time Jesus had come to visit her. She was five years old and kneeling alone in her little room. It suddenly filled with light and there was a beautiful Lady standing before her. "Who are you?" Catherine had asked, "and how did you get in here without opening the door?"

The Lady had answered, "I am the Mother of Jesus, your Redeemer. He wants you to give Him your heart."

Catherine had been so young then, she remembered, that she had not known quite what the Lady meant. "My heart?" she asked. "I don't know where it is, but if you can find it, yes, I would like to give it to Him."

Then the Lady had smiled and laid her hand over Catherine's heart. "There it is," she said, "and you give it to Him every time you obey cheerfully or suffer something for Him." It had been then that Jesus Himself appeared, as a boy about her own age. She never could forget how light the room had been, and the angels and saints that had filled it with songs from heaven. Our Lady had taken from her own finger a gold ring set with three pearls, which she put on Catherine's finger. "Now you belong to my Son," she said.

No one but Catherine could ever see the ring. She could see it shining there on her finger all the time, reminding her of Jesus' love. She had many chances to prove to Him that she loved Him, too, by obeying cheerfully and by suffering for Him.

She was thinking of all these things when suddenly there was another crash. There on the floor lay the pieces of one of their few plates. Catherine was both sorry and frightened. There seemed to be only one thing to do — she said a prayer for help, made the sign of the cross over the pieces; and there was the plate, whole again!

This was not the only time that Jesus helped His little friend. He was so happy to have someone who thought of

Across from her sat her little Friend from heaven.

Him and kept Him in her heart by prayer, that He often came to see her. He always appeared as a child of her own age. He would remind her that no matter how sad life on earth sometimes is, heaven is very happy.

There were many things to make Catherine sad. Her parents were so poor that she had almost starved to death when she was a baby. War had come to their part of the country, and had left their home a heap of ashes. Nothing would grow in the fields for years to come. Her father was a locksmith by trade, and since the war nobody needed any locks and he had no work. To earn a little bread, Catherine's mother had to work all day at the noisy loom, weaving heavy cloth to sell. Because they were worried and unhappy, Catherine's mother and father scolded and quarreled. The loom clacked all day, filling the house with noise. The little girl and her brother were often punished. They had to work very hard; and sometimes, too, they were hungry.

One day Catherine's parents quarreled and went away for awhile, leaving the little girl alone. She felt so sad that she could not do anything but cry; and when mealtime came, she sat down at the table and did not want to eat at all. Then she rubbed her eyes and smiled — for across from her sat her little Friend from heaven!

Another time when Catherine was learning to weave, she had made many mistakes and spoiled the cloth. She put her head down on the loom and cried. She heard a voice beside her saying, "Why do you cry?" It was her Friend again.

"Jesus, our hope!" she said. "We have no money, and father and mother are quarreling again. I am not any help to them, for I only spoil my work and make things worse than ever. I do not mind being poor, but I wish they would not quarrel."

"Here is a little coin," He said. "It will buy all you need for some time."

One day Catherine went visiting with a friend to a near-by city. There was in this town a house of the Preaching Friars, and Catherine wished to meet them. While they were talking to one of the priests, Catherine noticed a picture on the wall. "Who is that?" she asked.

"That is Saint Peter Martyr," said the priest. "He is a saint of our Order."

"I've seen him," said Catherine, "but I was not sure of his name."

"Seen him?" asked the priest. "You couldn't have, child. He has been dead for many years."

Catherine did not explain that Saint Peter Martyr had been one of the saints who came with our Lord and His Blessed Mother the time she was given the ring. She just said, "I am going to wear that habit some day, too."

The priest looked puzzled. "I am afraid that will be hard, unless you go away somewhere. There are no Dominican sisters near where you live."

"There will be, when I grow up," Catherine said.

Many times the saints appeared to Catherine when she was praying in her room. Saint Agnes, the little girl martyr, was her favorite. Often the saints who came to see her wore the black and white habit of the Preaching Friars. "Some day I will wear black and white myself," Catherine would say.

One day Catherine's mother had baked bread and she gave the little girl a piece of it to eat. There was nothing Catherine liked quite so much as fresh bread, so she went happily outdoors to eat it. She had gone only a few steps when she met a beggar girl. "An alms, for the love of God," begged the girl.

Catherine looked at the bread. It looked much too nice to give away, and Catherine was hungry herself. So she said, "Mother is baking, and if you ask her in a little while, I am sure she will give you a piece too."

Then as she went on down the street, her conscience began to hurt. "I needn't have been so selfish," she said to herself. "Jesus wouldn't like me to do that." She turned and ran back to the beggar girl. "I'm sorry," she said. "You can have mine."

The girl took only a small piece of the bread and gave the rest back to Catherine. "It tastes much better now than it did before," said Catherine to herself. "I wonder why?"

As Catherine grew older, she prayed more and more, and did many hard penances for sinners. As you might expect, there was someone who didn't like this very well, and that was the devil. It always bothers him to have people pray, but when those prayers succeed in stealing souls from him and sending them to heaven, then he really gets angry. Several very wicked people were saved at the last minute by Catherine's prayers, so the devil began thinking of ways to keep her from praying. First he appeared to her, ugly as he is, and tried to frighten her. She had one good answer to that; she made the sign of the cross and said, "Jesus, our hope!" so there was nothing for the evil spirit to do but run. Then he appeared to her in many different forms to give her good advice which she was wise enough not to take. When he saw even that was not doing any good to his cause, he began stirring up the people around town to talk about her.

The devil loves people who gossip, because they never say anything kind. So he went about among Catherine's neighbors and started them talking. "There are strange lights in her room at night," one neighbor would say. "Of course, I've never seen them myself, but I've heard about them." Another would answer, "She must be a witch. We had better have nothing to do with her." Soon everyone in town was avoiding Catherine. She did not mind very much because she liked to suffer for Jesus, but it would spoil her plans to be a Dominican if the Fathers should believe everything they heard about her. They would not want anyone in their Order who was as wicked as the neighbors said she was.

However, her faith was very strong, and finally she was allowed to wear the habit in her own home. From then until the time of her death her life was a long prayer. All day at the clacking loom she prayed as she wove the cloth to sell and help her parents. All night, or very nearly all night, she prayed in her room. She did great penances for sinners; and try as he might, the devil could not stop her.

Catherine's prayers were for all sinners, but most of all she prayed for soldiers. There was a war going on near by, and hundreds of soldiers were dying every day, with little or no time to get their souls ready for judgment. Many of those who might otherwise have been lost, owed the grace of dying happily to a little sister whom none of them had ever seen and few had heard of — Sister Catherine, who prayed for them to "Jesus, our hope."

Just as Catherine had said long ago, a convent for Dominican sisters was built in her little town. This and other prophecies came true, to show people she was very near to Jesus and that she knew some of His secrets of the future. Finally, even the people who had gossiped about her came to realize that she was a saint, and they came to her to ask for prayers.

They did not know, of course, of all the wonderful visits she had had with Jesus and His Blessed Mother and the saints. She did not tell them, either, about the ring set with pearls, which no one could see but herself. The only person she did tell about these great favors was her confessor. She asked him to tell about them after she was dead, so that people would glorify God. When Catherine died, after a long life of suffering and misunderstanding, he did tell about these things, and people were sorry they had talked so wickedly about her.

Blessed Catherine of Racconigi can help us to be patient, when we are tired or hungry or in need of money, or when people say things about us that are not true. We should ask her help in remembering — always — that Jesus is near us, watching over us and loving us, no matter how poor or how sad we might be. When we are very discouraged, it would be a good thing to remember the prayer she said so often, the tiny prayer of only three words that gave her so much help, "Jesus, our hope."

Blessed Sadoc reads the book of martyrs.

Hail, Holy Queen

IT WAS very dark in the chapel, because at the midnight Office only the glow of a few candles shone in tiny points of light on the altar and on the stand in the center aisle where the big prayer book was. Father Sadoc had closed his eyes and was listening carefully while one of the young novices read from the book the names of the martyrs whose feast would be kept the next day.

"One must be very brave to be a martyr," thought Father Sadoc. "It is easy to say that martyrdom is a quick way to heaven, but it is not easy to die. We should pray every day to be strong in our faith, so that if the time should ever come for us to be killed rather than deny our faith, we would be ready."

Brother Christopher, one of the novices, was thinking about martyrdom, too. But his thoughts were not exactly like those of Father Sadoc, for he was wishing that he *could* be a martyr. "It must be a very good way to go to heaven," he was thinking, as he listened to the novice reading. "Only a little while of suffering, and heaven forever. Sometimes I get very tired of doing the same old thing day after day, working hard to keep from losing my temper, and trying to be charitable. It would be much easier just to die for Christ. Of course, there isn't much chance of that here in Poland. There might have been when our Fathers first came here years ago, but there isn't now. It is too bad. I just never do have very good luck."

And just at that moment, the novice stopped reading, looked very hard at the book, and read out, "At Sandomir, the passion of forty-nine martyrs."

Sandomir! Why, that was their very own town! Father Sadoc opened his eyes and looked at the novice who was reading. Perhaps he heard it wrong, he thought, or maybe the novice had made a mistake as novices sometimes do. So he told the young man to please read it over again.

The novice looked harder than ever at the book and then read again, "At Sandomir, the passion of forty-nine martyrs."

Father Sadoc left his place at the back of the chapel and went to see for himself. No wonder the novice looked puzzled — for there on the page, in letters of bright gold, were the words he had read: "Forty-nine martyrs." He knew without counting them that there were exactly forty-nine in the house.

"My dear brothers," said Father Sadoc, "we are going to go to heaven tomorrow. God must have written that warning for us so that we could prepare to die well. There is nothing to be sad about, only great cause for happiness that God loves us so much. He will let us suffer for Him. Let us make our hearts ready to meet Him, tomorrow, at the judgment throne."

You may be sure that no one went to bed that night, for all were busy preparing their hearts for the death that they were sure would come to them the next day. Everyone went to confession and received his last Holy Communion; those who were priests said their Masses with great devotion, knowing that this would be the last time they should ever have the chance to say Mass.

Early in the morning there was a cry in the streets. "The Tartars are coming!" cried the frightened people. "They are almost at the gates of the city! We shall be killed!" For everyone *knew* that the wild Tartar tribes who rode down from the north had no mercy on anyone; they would steal and kill and burn when they broke into a city, and going away, leave it in ashes without a living person left in it. No wonder they were afraid!

Sandomir was quite well fortified, and as the soldiers had warning, they set about defending their city. There was at least a chance that they might drive off the invaders, although they were very much outnumbered. All day they fought bravely; but as evening came on, they began to be very much afraid. Father Sadoc and his brother priests had been busy all day hearing confessions and preparing the people to die if the Tartars should take the city. They had gone back to the convent to say the evening Office when word was passed around the city that someone had betrayed them and opened the gates to the Tartars.

Everyone in the convent was very calm, and ready for what would happen. Everyone, that is, but Brother Christopher. For as the hour of his death drew closer, and closer, he found that he was not the least bit anxious to die. The fact was that Brother Christopher was something like Saint Peter, who talked very bravely of dying for his Master until the time came to be tested — and then, he was very much afraid. He ran to Father Sadoc as the priests were returning from the city. "Father Sadoc!" he cried, "is it true that we are going to die?"

"Yes, Brother," said the priest. "Soon we will be before God. Surely that does not frighten you, my son?"

"Yes, it does, Father," admitted Brother Christopher.

"We should all fear the judgment, for we are all sinners," said Father Sadoc, "but you are prepared by a good confession, aren't you?"

"Yes, Father," replied the frightened brother.

"Then you may be sure that our Blessed Lady will be there to plead for you at the throne of God. Saint Dominic will be there, and our brothers, the martyrs of Hungary,

The Martyrs of Sandomir.

and many others. You will not go alone, for there are forty-nine of us; and, being brothers, we will go together. You must not be afraid," said Father Sadoc.

"But can't we *do* something?" begged poor Brother Christopher.

"Yes," said Father Sadoc, "there is something we can do. We can say our Office. Do not be afraid, Brother — we shall all pray for each other; and God will give you courage if you ask Him for it. Now go, and ring the bell for Office."

Brother Christopher was still very frightened as he watched the brothers coming into the chapel for Office. Try as he might, he could not keep from shivering at the thought of the Tartars. If the others were afraid — and they probably were — they hid it well; for they started to sing the Office as though nothing at all were wrong.

All the prayers of this beautiful evening Office were chosen to make us think of death. This is not to frighten anyone but to remind us at the evening of the day that life, too, will come to a close some day; and we will go through the dark night of death to meet God. Poor frightened Brother Christopher and the other young men who chanted the evening Office there in that chapel of long ago, must have thought a great deal as they sang so bravely:

"Brethren, be sober and watch, because your enemy
The devil, as a roaring lion, goes about seeking
Whom he may devour: whom resist ye, strong in faith. . . ."

"Strong in faith!" said Brother Christopher to himself. "I'm sorry to be such a coward, dear Lord. Help me to be strong!"

After the Confiteor, which all said together, the two choirs sang the verses from the Psalms which were to be said that day:

"He that dwelleth in the shelter of the Most High,
   And abideth in the shadow of the Almighty. . . ."

sang the first choir, and the second answered:

"Shall say to the Lord,
'Thou art my protector and my refuge!
My God, in whom I trust!' "

Brother Christopher glanced across the chapel at Father Sadoc, and saw that his face was shining as though he were very happy. "I ought to be happy, too," said the novice to himself. "If I just *did* trust God as much as I ought to!"

"With His pinions will He shelter thee,
   And under His wings thou shalt be secure,"

chanted the one choir.

"Like a shield His truth shall guard thee;
   Thou shalt not fear the terrors of the night,"

answered the other choir.

From the street there was a sound of shouting, the noise of heavy fighting, the screams of the injured. Smoke began to pour in at the windows of the convent, and still the choir chanted:

"He hath given his angels charge over thee,
   To keep thee in all thy ways:
They shall bear thee up in their hands,
   Lest thou dash thy foot against a stone."

From his place in the back of the chapel Father Sadoc looked down at the brothers who were chanting so bravely. "Dear Lord, give all of us courage to die well," he prayed. "Help poor Brother Christopher to be strong and faithful."

As if in answer to his thoughts, the choir chanted the words of our Lord on the cross:

"Into Thy hands, O Lord, I commend my spirit:
Alleluia,
For Thou hast redeemed us, Lord, God of truth,
Alleluia, Alleluia."

They could hear the outer doors breaking in as they formed into line for the procession to our Lady with which evening prayers always closed. Two young novices took their places carrying torches at the head of the procession, and behind them the community followed, two by two. They sang:

"Hail, Holy Queen! Hail, Mother of Mercy,
Our life, our sweetness, and our hope.
To thee we cry, poor banished children of Eve;
To thee we send up our sighs, mourning and
weeping in this valley of tears.
Turn then, most gracious Advocate, thine eyes of
mercy toward us. . . ."

As the brothers went singing down the chapel aisle, the Tartars met them and fell upon them with their swords. Father Sadoc and his brothers fell one by one, their white robes dyed red with the blood of martyrdom.

And what of Brother Christopher? He was so frightened, so the old legend says, that he broke out of line and ran up into the loft. There he lay trembling in fright; and he heard below him in the chapel the voices of his brothers, still singing the hymn to our Lady. One by one, the voices he knew so well stopped singing on earth as they went singing into heaven. Finally, Brother Christopher looked over the railing of the loft and saw a strange sight. There were golden crowns there in the air above the clouds of smoke. As he watched, the crowns came down gently, one by one, and rested on the heads of his martyred brothers. But one crown still hung there in the air; he looked and saw that all

[109]

the brothers were dead, and there was no one left to wear the other crown.

"It's mine!" sobbed Brother Christopher, "and they are all going to heaven without me. Oh, dear Lord, I am too much of a coward to die bravely — but *you* will help me! I give my life for You; now You must make me brave enough to wear that crown!"

The Tartars must have been surprised to see Brother Christopher walking bravely down out of the loft and into their midst. They fell upon him and killed him, too; and very soon the forty-ninth crown came to rest on the head of Brother Christopher, the martyr, who went happily off to heaven with his brothers.

Because of these martyrs of Sandomir, who went so bravely to their deaths singing a hymn to our Lady, it is still a custom to sing the "Hail, Holy Queen" around the bed of a dying Dominican, priest or sister. We cannot all die martyrs, and not all of us would have the courage to die for our faith. But death is always a last hard battle with the devil who wants to steal the soul; and, like those martyrs of long ago, it is wise to have our Lady near us when we die. That is why the brothers and sisters of Blessed Sadoc and the martyrs of Sandomir have kept the lovely custom of sending a brother or sister Dominican off to heaven with a song that is a prayer: Hail, Holy Queen!

Bibliography

Anneé Dominicaine (Lyon: X. Jevain, Imprimeur-Editeur, Rue Francoise-Dauphine 18, 1898).

Bullarium Ordinis FF. Praedicatorum, Ed. P. Antoninus Bremond, O.P. (Roma, 1729).

Catalogus Hagiographicus Ordinis Praedicatorum, P. Innocentius Taurisano, O.P. (Roma: Unio Typographica Manuzio, Via di Porta Salaria, 23–B, 1918).

Catholic Encyclopedia (New York: Robert Appleton and Co., 1911).

Dominicans, The, John Baptist Reeves, O.P. (Macmillan, 1930).

First Disciples of Saint Dominic, The, Very Rev. Victor F. O'Daniel, O.P. (Herder, 1928).

Golden Legend of Jacobus de Voragine, The, translated from Latin by Granger Ryan and Helmut Ripperger (Longmans, Green and Co., 1941).

Les Bienheureuses Dominicaines 1190–1577, D'Apres Des Documents Inédits, M. C. De Ganay (Paris: Librairie Academique).

Les Petits Bollandistes, Vies Des Saints, Msr. Paul Guérin (Paris: Bloud et Barral, Libraires, 18 Rue Cassette, 18, 1880).

Life of Saint Dominic, Most Rev. J. S. Alemany, O.P. (P. O'Shea, 1867).

Life of Saint Dominic, Bede Jarrett, O.P. (Burns, Oates and Washbourne, 1934).

Life of Saint Dominick, translated from the French of Father Henry Dominic Lacordaire by George Whitley Abraham (Dublin, 1851).

Lives of the Brethren, Fr. Placid Conway, O.P. (Burns, Oates and Washbourne, 1924).

[111]

Lives of the Dominican Saints, Dominican Fathers of the Province of Saint Joseph, 1940.

Lives of the Saints, Rev. Alban Butler (Sadlier, 1857).

Materials for a Life of Jacopo Da Varagine, Ernest Cushing Richardson (New York: The H. W. Wilson Co., 1935).

Pèlerinages Dominicaines, B. Kirsch et H. S. Roman, Societè Saint-Augustin (Paris: Descleé, De Brouwer & Cie., Rue Saint-Sulpice, 1920).

Raymond of Penafort, Thomas M. Schwertner, O.P., revised and edited by C. M. Antony (Milwaukee: The Bruce Publishing Co., 1935).

Religious Life, The, Bede Jarrett, O.P. (Burns, Oates and Washbourne, 1939).

Saint Dominic, Jean Guiraud, translated by Katherine de Mattos (Benziger, 1913).

Saints of the Rosary, Rev. T. A. Dyson, O.P. (New York: D. and J. Sadlier and Co., 1897).

Scriptores Ordinis Praedicatorum, Quetif et Echard, O.P. (Paris, 1719).

Short Lives of Dominican Saints: Sisters of Saint Catherine of Siena, Kegan Paul (London: Trench Trübner and Co., 1901).

Spirit of Saint Dominic, The, F. Humbert Clérissac, O.P. (Burns, Oates and Washbourne, 1939).

Spirit of the Dominican Order, The, Mother Frances Raphael Drane (Benziger, 1910).

Stars in Saint Dominic's Crown, Rev. T. A. Dyson, O.P. (New York: D. and J. Sadlier and Co., 1890).

Storia di S. Piero-Martire Di Verona, Fr. Pier-Tommaso Campana (Milano, 1741).

Vita De I Santi E Beati, Cosi Huomini, Come Donne Del Sacro Ordine De Frati Predicatori, Fra Serafino Razzi (Firenze: Bartolomeo Sermartelli, 1777).

Within the Golden Gates, Rev. T. A. Dyson, O.P. (New York: D. and J. Sadlier and Co., 1894).